Practice Workbook

Boston, Massachusetts
Upper Saddle River, New Jersey

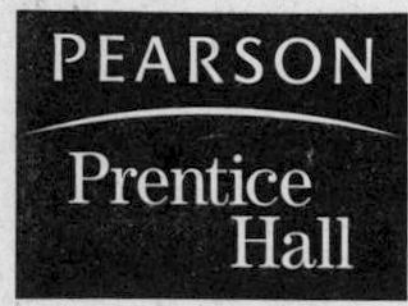

ISBN 0-13-036002-3

15 16 17 18 19 20 21 22 23   11 10 09 08 07

Es bueno, son buenos

A. Write the plural of each of the following adjectives.

1. joven ______
2. simpático ______
3. guapa ______
4. inteligente ______
5. atrevida ______

B. Now, fill in the missing masculine or feminine form of each adjective.

M	F
trabajador	
	deportista
paciente	
	alta
viejo	

C. Now, write an adjective to describe the people in the drawings below. Follow the model.

Modelo *graciosos*

1. ______

3. ______

2. ______

4. ______

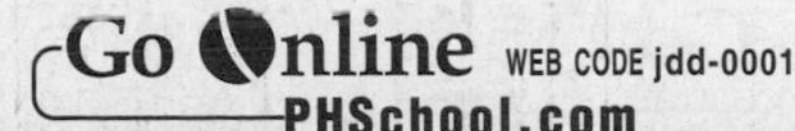

WEB CODE jdd-0001

Somos así

A. Fill in the chart below for the verb **ser**.

	sois

B. Now, write complete sentences using the cues provided and the verb **ser**. Don't forget to make the adjective agree with the noun. Follow the model.

Modelo Juan / impaciente *Juan es impaciente*.

1. Isabel / inteligente ______.
2. Sara y Ana / estudioso ______.
3. la señora García / sociable ______.
4. los estudiantes / serio ______.
5. mi familia y yo / artístico ______.
6. la chica / talentoso ______.
7. nosotras / joven ______.
8. tú / bajo ______.
9. el profesor / gracioso ______.
10. yo / reservado ______.

Go Online WEB CODE jdd-0002
PHSchool.com

Explorar el mundo

Read the descriptions below and tell what each person's nationality is. Follow the model.

Modelo Felipe vive en Europa. Es de Madrid, España.
Es español ____________.

1. A ti te gusta la ciudad. Eres de Buenos Aires, Argentina.
   ______________________________.
2. Ramiro es de la capital de Puerto Rico.
   ______________________________.
3. Pedro y yo somos de la misma ciudad, Santo Domingo, en la República Dominicana.
   ______________________________.
4. Maricarmen y Elena son de Santiago, la capital de Chile.
   ______________________________.
5. No soy colombiano, soy de México.
   ______________________________.
6. Ana Lisette es de la Ciudad de Guatemala.
   ______________________________.
7. Luis y Ramón son de la Ciudad de Panamá.
   ______________________________.
8. Inés es de Perú, pero vive en Paraguay ahora.
   ______________________________.
9. Livan y yo vivimos en Miami, pero somos de Cuba.
   ______________________________.
10. Tú vives en los Estados Unidos, pero eres de Colombia.
    ______________________________.
11. Leydin es de la capital de Costa Rica.
    ______________________________.
12. Yo soy de San Antonio, Texas.
    ______________________________.

El horario

A. Read as Anita describes her daily schedule. Fill in the present tense forms of the verbs in parentheses.

A las seis de la mañana yo ______________ (correr) al parque. Mi familia ______________ (vivir) cerca del parque, entonces ______________ (correr) sólo tres kilómetros cada mañana. Cuando ______________ (regresar) a mi casa mi familia y yo ______________ (desayunar). Luego voy a la escuela.

Durante el día ______________ (pasar) tiempo con mis amigos. Por la tarde ellos ______________ (practicar) deportes pero yo no. Soy miembro de una banda musical con mi hermano. Él ______________ (tocar) la guitarra y yo ______________ (cantar). Nosotros ______________ (practicar) todos los días después de las clases.

Por la noche yo ______________ (escuchar) música o ______________ (bailar) en mi cuarto. Mis padres ______________ (leer) revistas o ______________ (ver) la tele, y mi hermano ______________ (montar) en monopatín con sus amigos.

B. Now, answer the following questions about your own daily activities.

1. ¿Vives cerca de un parque? ¿Corres al parque todos los días por la mañana?
____
____
2. ¿Pasas tiempo con tus amigos en la escuela? ¿Y después de las clases?
____
____
3. ¿Practicas deportes? ¿Cuáles deportes practicas? Si no practicas deportes, ¿qué más haces? ______________________________
____
____
4. ¿Cuándo comes la cena con tu familia? ¿Y el desayuno?
____
____
5. ¿Adónde vas los fines de semana? ¿Qué haces allí? ______________
____
____

Go Online WEB CODE jdd-0004 PHSchool.com

Nombre ______________________ Hora ______

Fecha ______________________ Practice Workbook **1A–A**

¿Qué haces en la escuela?

A. Identify the items found in your classroom.

1. Hago mi tarea en la ______________________.
2. La profesora abre la ______________________.
3. Alicia mira el ______________________ para saber qué hora es.
4. No puedes escribir con este lápiz. Necesitas un ______________________.
5. Me gustan los colores del ______________________.
6. Para escribir bien, necesitas usar un ______________________.

B. Read each description of school subjects below, and write which subject each one describes.

1. ______________________ Aprendemos sobre la computadora.
2. ______________________ Hay cuadros bonitos en los libros.
3. ______________________ Necesitan una calculadora.
4. ______________________ A Laura le gusta estudiar las plantas.
5. ______________________ Juan juega al tenis.
6. ______________________ Aprendemos de nuestro país y los países del mundo.

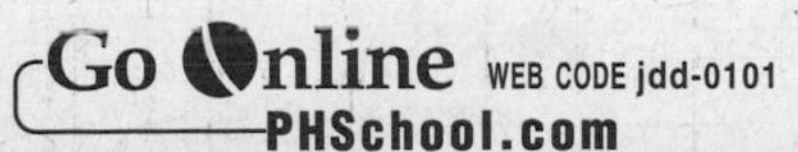

A ver si recuerdas...

¿Qué tienes que hacer?

A. Use an expression with the verb **tener** to tell about the following people using the information given. Follow the model.

Modelo Martín / hacer la tarea *Martín tiene que hacer la tarea*.

1. Ellos / comer ____________________.
2. Tú / ir a la lección de piano ____________________.
3. Nosotros / ir a la escuela ____________________.
4. La profesora / enseñar la clase ____________________.
5. Yo / ir de compras ____________________.
6. Mis amigos / beber leche ____________________.
7. Elena y yo / usar la computadora ____________________.

B. Fill in the mini-conversations with the correct form of the verbs given.

1. (traer)

   —¿Adónde ____________ (tú) esos pasteles?

   —____________ estos pasteles a la mesa.

2. (hacer)

   —¿Qué ____________ (tú) después de las clases?

   —____________ la tarea después de las clases.

3. (poner)

   —¿Qué ____________ (Uds.) en la mesa?

   —____________ los tenedores, las cucharas y los cuchillos en la mesa.

4. (tener)

   —¿Cuántos años ____________ (tú)?

   —Yo ____________ dieciséis años.

5. (poner)

   —¿Usted ____________ la mesa por la mañana o por la tarde?

   —____________ la mesa por la tarde.

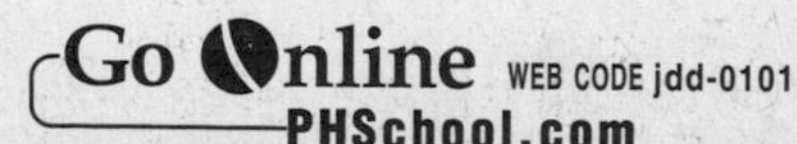

¿Qué hacen los estudiantes?

A. Use the pictures to figure out what each student brings to class.

1. Emilio trae ______________________.
2. La profesora trae ______________________.
3. Yo traigo mi ______________________.
4. Tú traes ______________________.
5. Los estudiantes traen todos ______________________ para la clase.

B. Now, write the phrase that corresponds to what students do during the school day. Follow the model.

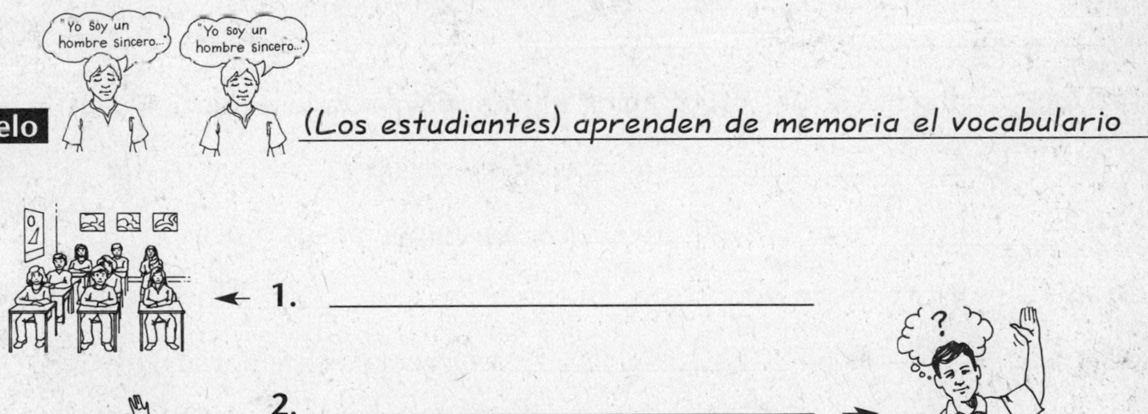

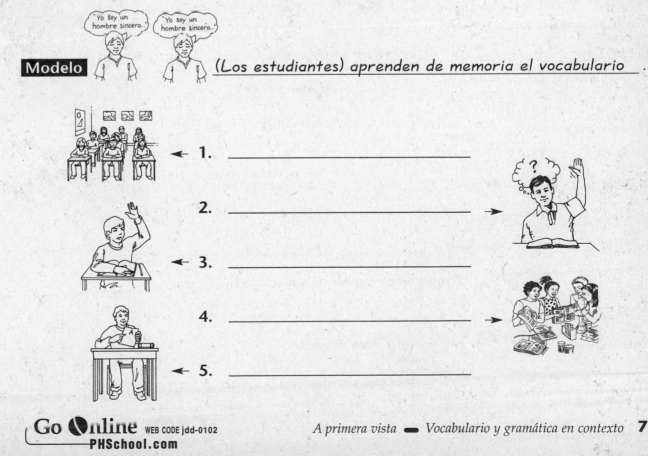

Modelo *(Los estudiantes) aprenden de memoria el vocabulario*.

1. ______________________
2. ______________________

3. ______________________
4. ______________________
5. ______________________

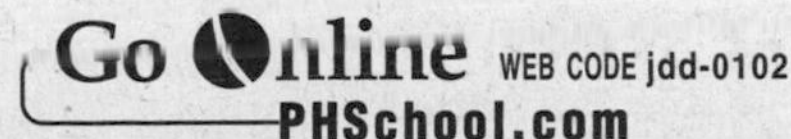

Las reglas

A. Complete the following rules with **hay que** or **se prohíbe** to show your teacher that you know what is expected of you.

1. ______________________ almorzar en la sala de clase.
2. ______________________ respetar a los demás.
3. ______________________ entregar la tarea a tiempo.
4. ______________________ ir al armario durante las clases.
5. ______________________ contestar las preguntas del profesor.

B. Fill in the blanks below with words from the bank.

aprendieron	**discutir**	**asientos**	**palabra**
entiendo	**explicar**	**repetir**	**empieza**

Son las dos y media de la tarde y los estudiantes entran en la clase. Todos pasan a sus

________________. *La clase* ________________.

PROFESOR: ¡Buenas tardes! Hoy vamos a hablar del poeta José Martí. Quiero ________________ su obra *Versos sencillos.*

ROSANA: Profesor, no ________________ este poema. Es difícil.

VÍCTOR: Estoy de acuerdo. ¿Usted puede ________________ qué quiere decir?

PROFESOR: ¿Ustedes no ________________ el poema de memoria?

ROSANA: No, profesor, es muy difícil de entender.

PROFESOR: Entonces vamos a ________________ cada ________________ todos los días para que ustedes aprendan todo de memoria.

ESTUDIANTES: ¡Uf!

PROFESOR: A ver... "Yo soy un hombre sincero..."

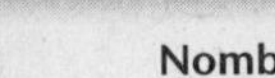

¿Qué tienes que hacer?

A. Your teacher is telling you about good and bad ways to behave in the classroom. Complete his thought with words from your vocabulary. Each dash represents a letter of the word.

1. Los chicos deben ___ ___ ___ ___ ___ e r al profesor como el Sr. Ríos.
   (13 18 3 18 13 12 4)
2. Los estudiantes malos siempre llegan ___ ___ r ___ e a la clase.
   (2 6 4 9 12)
3. Si un estudiante quiere ir al ___ r ___ ___ r ___ ___, le digo que no.
   (6 4 11 6 4 10 18)
4. Se ___ r ___ ___ í ___ e ir al armario durante la clase.
   (14 4 18 17 29 15 12)
5. ___ ___ ___ ___ e tiene el libro. ¿Por qué?
   (3 6 9 10 12)
6. Hay que estar en el ___ ___ ___ e ___ ___ ___ cuando la clase empieza.
   (6 1 10 12 3 2 18)
7. Para la clase de español, tenemos que ir al

   ___ ___ b ___ r ___ ___ ___ r ___ ___ cada semana.
   (5 6 15 18 4 6 2 18 4 10 18)
8. Esteban, ¿quiere Ud. dar un d ___ ___ ___ ___ r ___ ___ sobre las reglas de la clase?
   (9 10 1 13 20 4 1 18)
9. Cada semestre Uds. tienen que hacer un ___ r ___ ___ e ___ ___ ___ para
   (14 4 18 19 12 13 2 18)

   esta clase, como un informe o un discurso.

B. Now, using the coded letters from above, fill in the blanks to reveal another rule of the class.

"___ ___ ___ q ___ ___ ___ ___ ___ ___ ___ ___ ___ ___ ___
(17 6 19 26 20 12 14 4 12 1 2 6 4 5 12)

___ ___ ___ ___ ___ ___ ó ___ ___ ___ ___ ___ ___ f ___ ___ ___ ___"
(6 2 12 3 13 10 30 3 6 5 14 4 18 22 12 1 18 4)

Nombre ______ Hora ______

Fecha ______ Practice Workbook **1A–4**

La estudiante ideal

Read the following progress reports of two students in the same class, then answer the questions below.

Elena Educada

- siempre le presta atención al profesor
- siempre llega a tiempo y está en su asiento cuando la clase empieza
- saca una "A" en todos los proyectos y exámenes
- siempre entrega la tarea a tiempo

Teresa Traviesa

- siempre está jugando y no prestando atención en la clase
- siempre llega tarde a clase
- saca malas notas en los exámenes y no hace ningún proyecto
- nunca entrega la tarea

1. ¿Cuál estudiante saca mejores notas?

   ______.

2. En tu opinión, ¿cuál estudiante contesta más preguntas en clase?

   ______.

3. En tu opinión, ¿cuál estudiante conoce bien las reglas de la clase?

   ______.

4. Si la clase empieza a las nueve ¿quién está en su asiento a las nueve y quién llega a las nueve y cinco?

   ______.

5. En tu opinión, ¿quién es la mejor estudiante? ¿Por qué?

   ______

   ______

   ______.

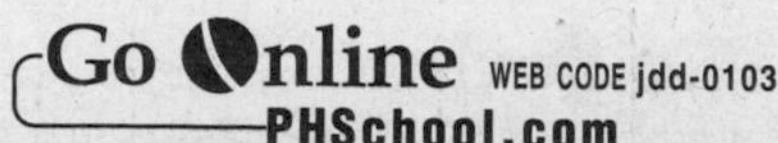

Realidades 2 Nombre ____________ Hora ____________

Capítulo 1A Fecha ____________ Practice Workbook **1A–5**

En la escuela hoy

Complete these sentences by choosing the correct verb in parentheses and writing the appropriate form in the space provided.

1. (repetir / pedir) Yo ______________ la palabra.
2. (querer / almorzar) Uds. ______________ en la sala de clases.
3. (jugar / entender) ¿Tú no ______________ la lección?
4. (preferir / servir) María ______________ llegar tarde hoy.
5. (dormir / servir) Ellos ______________ unas galletas.
6. (jugar / dormir) Ud. ______________ al fútbol americano.
7. (empezar / almorzar) Yo ______________ el informe.
8. (pensar / entender) Tú ______________ entregar la tarea mañana.
9. (pedir / entender) Los estudiantes ______________ ayuda después de la clase.
10. (costar / dormir) Nosotros ______________ en la sala de clases.
11. (costar / repetir) ¿Cuánto ______________ las tijeras?
12. (servir / querer) Yo ______________ jugar al golf con ustedes.

Realidades 2

Capítulo 1A

Nombre ______ Hora ______

Fecha ______ Practice Workbook **1A–6**

Algunos, sí

A. Add the correct form of **ninguno** or **alguno** to complete these sentences.

1. Hoy no tengo ningun clase.
2. Él no trae ninguna grapadora.
3. Esta semana no hacemos ningun proyecto.
4. algunas chicos quieren hacer una pregunta cada día.
5. Felipe sabe algunas reglas, pero no todas.
6. —¿Hay un profesor aquí?

   —No, no hay un profesor.
7. —¿María Rosa entrega todas la tareas?

   —No, pero entrega algunas.
8. Vamos a escuchar algunos discurso.

B. Rewrite the sentences in the negative using negative words. Follow the model.

Modelo Alguien llega. *No llega nadie.*

1. Alguien va al laboratorio. Nadie va al laboratorio
2. Ella presta atención también. Ella presta
3. Aprenden algo de memoria. ______
4. Hay algunas sillas en la sala. ______
5. Siempre llevas el carnet de identidad. ______

Go Online WEB CODE jdd-0105 PHSchool.com

Realidades 2 Nombre Hora

Capítulo 1A Fecha Practice Workbook **1A–7**

¡Qué problemas en la escuela!

Write out each sentence below to tell about problems in school. Follow the model.

Modelo Carlos / entender / nada

Carlos no entiende nada.

1. los estudiantes / pedir ayuda / nunca

2. yo / querer hacer el proyecto / nunca

3. tú / querer hacer el proyecto / tampoco

   tu no quieres hacer el proyecto tampoco

4. nosotros / dar un discurso / ningún

   nosotros no damos un discurso ninguno

5. el profesor / repetir las instrucciones / nunca

   el profesor no repetea ninguna las instrucciones

6. los estudiantes / llegar tarde / siempre

   los estudiantes llegan tarde siempre.

7. la profesora / conocer / estudiante de la clase / ningún

8. alguien / ir al armario / cada dos minutos

   alguien

9. mis amigos y yo / almorzar en la clase / siempre

   mis amigos y yo almorzaces en la clase siempre

10. tú / traer los materiales a clase / nunca

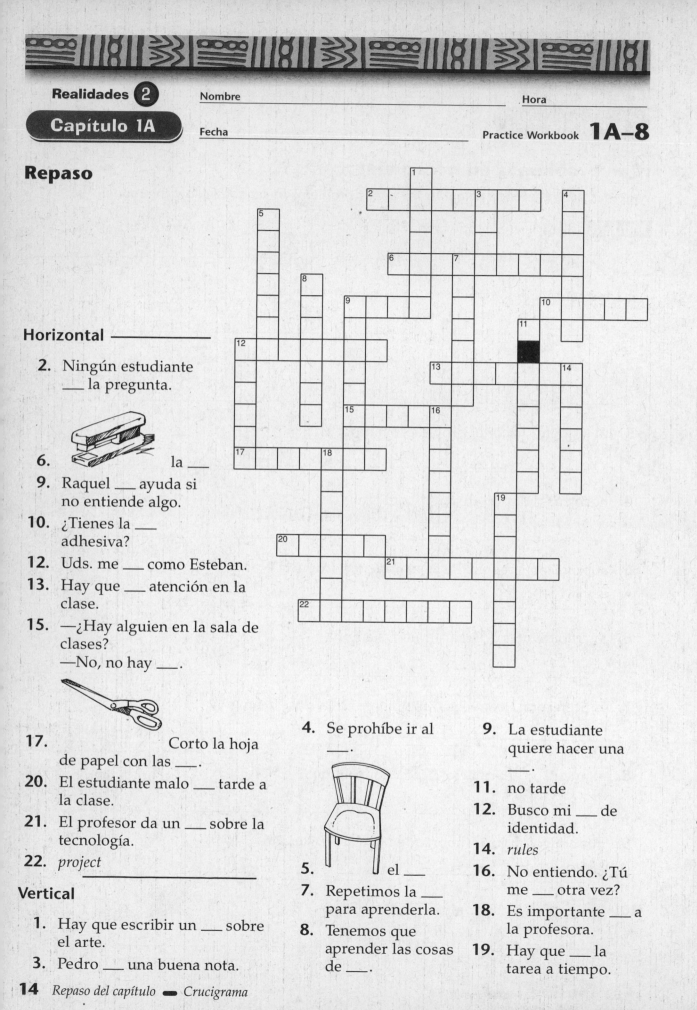

Nombre ______ Hora ______

Fecha ______ Practice Workbook **1A–8**

Repaso

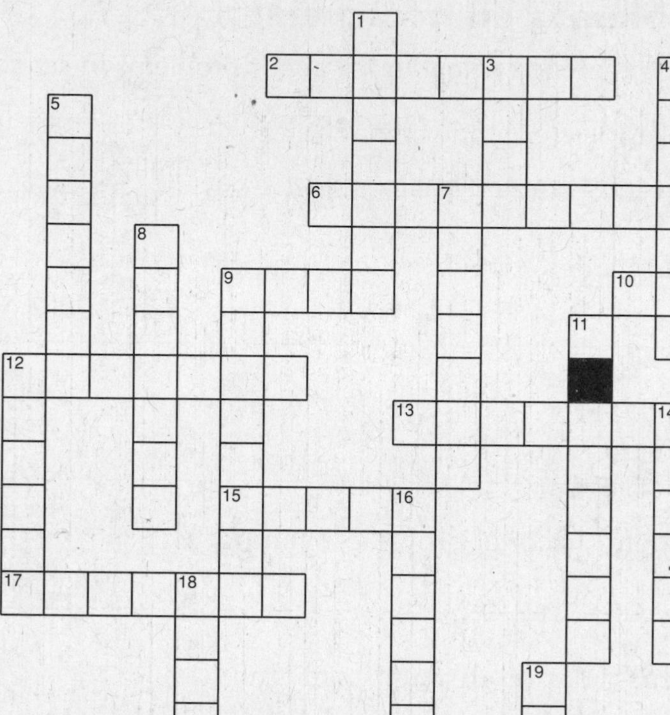

Horizontal

2. Ningún estudiante ___ la pregunta.
6.  la ___
9. Raquel ___ ayuda si no entiende algo.
10. ¿Tienes la ___ adhesiva?
12. Uds. me ___ como Esteban.
13. Hay que ___ atención en la clase.
15. —¿Hay alguien en la sala de clases?
—No, no hay ___.
17. 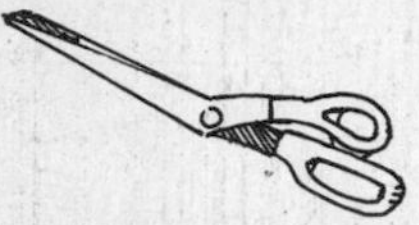 Corto la hoja de papel con las ___.
20. El estudiante malo ___ tarde a la clase.
21. El profesor da un ___ sobre la tecnología.
22. *project*

Vertical

1. Hay que escribir un ___ sobre el arte.
3. Pedro ___ una buena nota.
4. Se prohíbe ir al ___.
5.  el ___
7. Repetimos la ___ para aprenderla.
8. Tenemos que aprender las cosas de ___.
9. La estudiante quiere hacer una ___.
11. no tarde
12. Busco mi ___ de identidad.
14. *rules*
16. No entiendo. ¿Tú me ___ otra vez?
18. Es importante ___ a la profesora.
19. Hay que ___ la tarea a tiempo.

Nombre ________ Hora ________

Fecha ________ Practice Workbook **1A–9**

Organizer

I. Vocabulary

Materials

Activities in the classroom

Rules: Hay que

Se prohíbe

II. Grammar

1. Give the present tense forms of these verbs:

poder | **pedir**

2. Make a list of five negative words. What are their affirmative counterparts?

Negative Words	Affirmative Words
1.	
2.	
3.	
4.	
5.	

Nombre ______________________ Hora ______________

Fecha ______________________ Practice Workbook **1B–A**

A ver si recuerdas...

¿Qué quieren hacer después de la escuela?

Add the missing infinitives to tell what these people want to do after school and where they want to go by using the art as clues. Follow the model.

Modelo Yo quiero ___*leer*___ un libro en la ___*biblioteca*___.

1. Mis amigos quieren ____________ al béisbol en el ____________.

2. Teresa quiere ____________ la computadora en ____________.

3. Mi hermana quiere ____________ la guitarra en un ____________.

4. Tú quieres ____________ pesas en el ____________.

5. Uds. quieren ____________ como voluntarios para la ____________.

6. Elena quiere ____________ tiempo con los amigos en el ____________.

7.  Nosotros queremos ____________ de compras al ____________.

Go Online WEB CODE jdd-0111
PHSchool.com

A ver si recuerdas...

¿Adónde van ustedes?

A. Tell where these people are going by completing each of the following sentences with the correct form of the verb **ir**.

1. Mis padres __________ a la iglesia.
2. Yo __________ a casa.
3. Los niños __________ al parque.
4. Tú __________ a la biblioteca.
5. Mi abuela __________ al centro comercial.
6. Luis __________ a la piscina.
7. Alicia y yo __________ al restaurante.
8. Ud. __________ al trabajo.

B. Answer the following questions in complete sentences, using the art to help you.

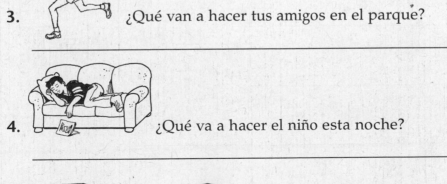

1. ¿Qué van a hacer Uds. después de las clases?

____.

2. ¿Qué vas a hacer este fin de semana?

____.

3. ¿Qué van a hacer tus amigos en el parque?

____.

4. ¿Qué va a hacer el niño esta noche?

____.

5. ¿Qué vas a hacer con tus amigos esta tarde?

____.

Nombre ______________________ Hora ____________

Fecha ______________________ Practice Workbook **1B–1**

¿Qué quieres ser?

A. Look at the drawings below and say what each person wants to do as an extracurricular activity.

1. A Tomás le gusta ______.
   Quiere ser miembro del club de ______________________.
2. A Mariana le gusta ______.
   Quiere hacer ______________________.
3. A Manolo le gusta ______.
   Quiere ser miembro del equipo de ______________________.
4. A Susana le gusta ______.
   Quiere ser miembro del club de ______________________.
5. A Plácido le gusta ______.
   Quiere ser miembro de la ______________________.

B. Look at the drawings and tell what each of these students is.

1. Juan es ______________________.
2. Marta es ______________________.
3. Luis y Patricia son ______________________.
4. Claudia es ______________________.
5. Laura y Angélica son ______________________.

Go Online WEB CODE jdd-0112
PHSchool.com

Después de las clases

Angélica and Lola are talking about extracurricular activities. Complete their conversation with words from the word bank.

sé	participas	vuelvo
artes	asistir	equipo
crear	reunión	piscina
oportunidad		

LOLA: Hoy a las tres hay una _______________ del club de computadoras. ¿Quieres _______________?

ALICIA: Lo siento, pero no puedo. Hoy después de las clases _______________ a casa para hacer la tarea.

LOLA: ¡Qué lástima!

ALICIA: Sí, porque me gustan mucho las computadoras. Quiero aprender a _______________ una página Web.

LOLA: ¿En qué actividades extracurriculares _______________ tú?

ALICIA: Soy miembro del _______________ de natación. ¿Y tú?

LOLA: Practico el karate. Me gustan mucho las _______________ marciales. Yo no _______________ nadar muy bien.

ALICIA: Tengo una idea. ¿Por qué no vienes a la _______________ conmigo el sábado? Yo te enseño.

LOLA: ¡Qué buena idea! Es la _______________ perfecta de empezar a nadar bien. ¡Hasta el sábado!

Nuestra actividades

Write the logical conclusion to each of these statements about students' interests and activities by selecting expressions from the word bank.

toma lecciones de guitarra	**es miembro del equipo de vóleibol**
ensaya hoy	**gana un premio**
vuelve a casa	**graba canciones**
tiene interés en el karate	**canta en el coro**
hace una búsqueda	**es animador**

1. A Carlos le gustan las artes marciales. Por eso, ______________________________.
2. A Isabel le gusta tocar música. Por eso, ______________________________.
3. La banda tiene un concierto mañana. Por eso, ______________________________.
4. Ricardo tiene una voz muy bonita. Por eso, ______________________________.
5. A Rosa le gustan los deportes. Por eso, ______________________________.
6. Felipe es el mejor jugador de la liga. Por eso, ______________________________.
7. Samuel tiene mucha tarea hoy. Por eso, ______________________________.
8. A Carmen le gusta escuchar música. Por eso, ______________________________.

Estos estudiantes hacen muchas cosas

Look at the sign-up list for school clubs. Based on their descriptions, which club do you think each student will sign up for? Follow the model.

Modelo A Ana le gusta tocar el piano.
Ana quiere ser miembro de la orquesta.

1. Pedro es deportista y le gusta patinar.

____

2. A Paulina le gusta jugar a los bolos.

____

3. A Héctor le gusta el ajedrez.

____

4. A Lourdes le gusta sacar fotos.

____

5. Iván es un buen músico.

____

6. Tina es animadora y quiere hacer algo similar.

____

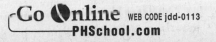

Nombre ____________ Hora ____________

Fecha ____________

Las actividades en nuestra escuela

José Luis is explaining things about the school to a new student. Use comparisons with **tan ... como** or **tanto(a) ... como** to find out what he says. Follow the models.

Modelo el karate / ser popular / el ajedrez
El karate es tan popular como el ajedrez.

clubes / hay en nuestra escuela/ equipos
Hay tantos clubes en nuestra escuela como equipos.

1. el club de ajedrez / tener reuniones / el club de computadoras
____

2. la natación / ser popular / el hockey
____

3. los miembros de la banda / ser talentoso / los miembros del coro
____

4. el periódico de la escuela / tener fotógrafas / fotógrafos
____

5. la música de la banda / ser bonita / la música de la orquesta
____

6. la orquesta / tener músicos / la banda
____

7. la cantante / cantar canciones / el cantante
____

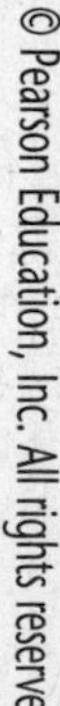

¿Sabes a quién conozco?

Ramón wants to join the school band but doesn't know the director. Complete the following conversation between Ramón and Susana with the correct forms of **saber** and **conocer** to find out who the director is.

Ramón ____________________ tocar el piano. Él quiere ser miembro de la banda, pero no ____________________ al director. Decide hablar con su amiga Susana.

RAMÓN: Oye, Susana, ¿____________________ quién es el director de la banda?

SUSANA: Sí, ______________ quién es. Es la profesora Durán. La ____________________ muy bien.

RAMÓN: ¿Tú ____________________ si necesitan más miembros en la banda?

SUSANA: ¿Por qué? ¿Quieres ser miembro de la banda? ¿Qué instrumento ____________________ tocar?

RAMÓN: Toco el piano. Mi amigo Paco y yo ____________________ la música de los artistas principales de la música clásica.

SUSANA: Fantástico. En la banda ahora nadie ____________________ tocar el piano. Ustedes ____________________ a varios miembros de la banda, ¿verdad?

RAMÓN: Sí, ____________________ a Miguel y a Rosa María. Gracias, Susana. Voy a buscar a la profesora Durán.

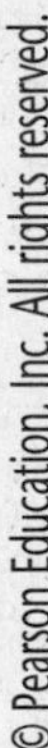

Nombre ____________ Hora ____________

Fecha ____________ Practice Workbook **1B–7**

Parece que fue ayer...

You are reporting for your school on the activities of various students. Fill in the following question and answer sessions using the clues given. Follow the models.

Modelo jugar al golf / Carmen, ¿*cuánto tiempo hace que juegas al golf*?
Hace cinco años que juego al golf.

tres años / Sergio, ¿cuánto tiempo hace que estudias inglés?
Hace tres años que estudio inglés.

1. jugar al ajedrez / Juan, ¿____________?

   Hace cinco años que juego al ajedrez contigo.
2. ocho meses / Julia y Carlos, ¿cuánto tiempo hace que usan la computadora?

   ____________.
3. un año / Edgardo, ¿cuánto tiempo hace que eres miembro del equipo de básquetbol?

   ____________.
4. tomar lecciones de piano / Elisa, ¿____________?

   Hace cuatro años que tomo lecciones de piano.
5. seis meses / Muchachos, ¿cuánto tiempo hace que trabajan en la tienda de electrodomésticos?

   ____________.
6. cantar en el coro / Andrea, ¿____________?

   Hace dos días que canto en el coro.
7. una semana / Jacinta y Jasmín, ¿cuánto tiempo hace que ustedes van al ensayo para la orquesta?

   ____________.

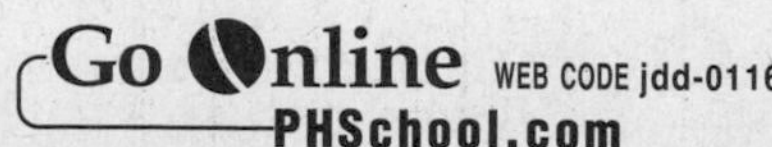

Repaso

Horizontal

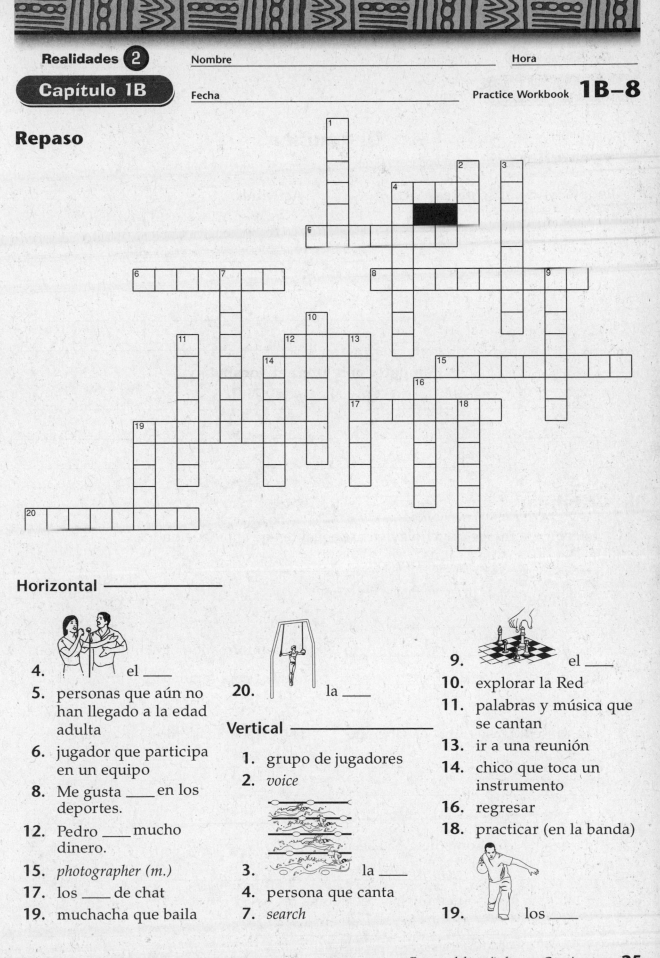

4. el ____
5. personas que aún no han llegado a la edad adulta
6. jugador que participa en un equipo
8. Me gusta ____ en los deportes.
12. Pedro ____ mucho dinero.
15. *photographer (m.)*
17. los ____ de chat
19. muchacha que baila
20. la ____

Vertical

1. grupo de jugadores
2. *voice*
3.  la ____
4. persona que canta
7. *search*
9. el ____
10. explorar la Red
11. palabras y música que se cantan
13. ir a una reunión
14. chico que toca un instrumento
16. regresar
18. practicar (en la banda)
19.  los ____

Nombre ______ Hora ______

Fecha ______ Practice Workbook **1B–9**

Organizer

I. Vocabulary

People who participate in activities | **Activities**

______ ______

______ ______

______ ______

______ ______

______ ______

Computer and Internet vocabulary

______ ______

______ ______

______ ______

II. Grammar

1. To compare things or people that are equal to one another, you use ______ + adjective + ______.
   To say *as much as* or *as many as*, you use ______ + noun + ______.
2. Use the verb ______ to talk about information or activities that you know. Use the verb ______ to talk about familiarity with people, places, or things.
3. The present tense forms of **saber** are: The present tense forms of **conocer** are:
   ______ ______ ______ ______
   ______ ______ ______ ______
   ______ ______ ______ ______
4. To ask how long something has been going on, say:
   ______
5. To tell how long something has been going on, say:
   ______

Go Online WEB CODE jdd-0118
PHSchool.com

A ver si recuerdas...

¿Qué ropa llevamos?

A. Use the pictures as cues and decide what article of clothing is appropriate for each event or description.

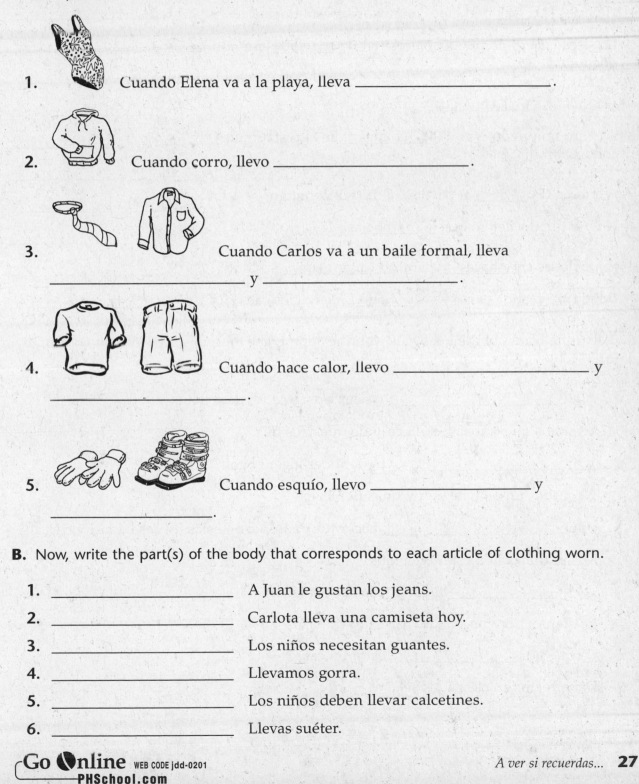

1. Cuando Elena va a la playa, lleva ______________________.

2. Cuando corro, llevo ______________________.

3. Cuando Carlos va a un baile formal, lleva ______________________ y ______________________.

4. Cuando hace calor, llevo ______________________ y ______________________.

5. Cuando esquío, llevo ______________________ y ______________________.

B. Now, write the part(s) of the body that corresponds to each article of clothing worn.

1. ______________________ A Juan le gustan los jeans.
2. ______________________ Carlota lleva una camiseta hoy.
3. ______________________ Los niños necesitan guantes.
4. ______________________ Llevamos gorra.
5. ______________________ Los niños deben llevar calcetines.
6. ______________________ Llevas suéter.

Realidades 2 | Nombre ______ | Hora ______

Capítulo 2A | Fecha ______ | Practice Workbook **2A–B**

A ver si recuerdas...

Van a invitarnos

A. Read the following conversations and change the underlined verbs to their correct form.

—¿Puedes (1) vas al cine con nosotros esta noche?

—Lo siento, pero no puedo. Necesito (2) arreglo mi dormitorio.

—¿Te gustaría (3) cenamos con nosotros?

—Sí, pero no puedo. Voy a (4) coméis en el restaurante con mi familia.

—¿Quieres (5) voy al partido de fútbol conmigo?

—No, no puedo. Tengo que (6) trabajas.

—¿Qué debes (7) haces para (8) mantiene la salud?

—Debo (9) como bien y (10) hago ejercicios cada día.

1. ______
2. ______
3. ______
4. ______
5. ______
6. ______
7. ______
8. ______
9. ______
10. ______

B. Fill in the blanks of the questions with the appropriate missing words in their correct forms.

1. ¿Qué ______ hacer Uds. este fin de semana?

   Tenemos que trabajar en la casa de nuestros tíos.

2. ¿Qué ______ para poder jugar al golf?

   Necesitas un palo de golf y unas pelotas.

3. ¿Qué ______ hacer tus padres si no estás en casa a las once?

   Mis padres van a estar enojados.

4. ¿______ jugar al béisbol mañana?

   Lo siento, pero no puedo. Necesito trabajar.

5. ¿A qué hora ______ estar en casa?

   Debes estar en casa a las seis.

¿Qué hace por la mañana?

A. Help Alicia describe what she does each morning as part of her daily routine by filling in the missing words.

1. Me ______ a las ocho. ¡Pero siempre quiero dormir más!
2. Me ______ de la cama.
3. Me ______ los dientes.
4. Me ______. No paso mucho tiempo en la ducha.
5. Me ______ el pelo con el secador.
6. Luego me ______ el pelo con el gel.
7. Me ______. Quiero llevar una blusa y falda hoy.
8. Me ______ agua de colonia.

B. Read the clues below. Then, write the vocabulary word that best fits each description.

1. Otra manera de decir "ponerse ropa" ______
2. No es después de ______
3. Es sinónimo de "usar una toalla" ______
4. Donde vas para cortarte el pelo ______
5. El antónimo de levantarse de la cama ______
6. Las joyas pueden ser de oro o de esto ______

Una conversación

Nidia and Diana are getting ready for their dates. Complete their conversation logically.

NIDIA: Tengo una _c_ ___ ___ ___ con Vicente esta noche. Vamos a un baile formal y elegante.

DIANA: Y yo salgo con mi novio Ramón. Vamos al cine. ¿Qué vas a llevar?

NIDIA: Mi vestido azul y unas _j_ ___ _y_ ___ ___ como aretes y un collar.

Me encantan los bailes ___ ___ ___ _g_ ___ ___ ___ _e_ ___.

DIANA: Ahora ___ _e_ _d_ _u_ ___ ___ ___ ___. Luego _m_ ___ _p_ ___ ___ ___ ___ las uñas.

NIDIA: Yo también debo ___ ___ ___ ___ _r_ me la cara y después, secarme el pelo con el ___ ___ ___ _a_ ___ ___ ___. ¿Sabes dónde está?

DIANA: Aquí está. ¿Puedo pedir _p_ ___ ___ ___ ___ ___ ___ ___ _s_ tus aretes de oro?

NIDIA: Ay chica, yo necesito esos aretes esta noche.

DIANA: Bueno, yo llevo mis aretes de ___ ___ ___ _t_ ___ entonces y mi collar.

NIDIA: De acuerdo.

Go Online WEB CODE jdd-0202 PHSchool.com

Nombre ______________________ Hora ______________

Fecha ______________________ Practice Workbook **2A–3**

Tenemos que salir

One of your friends is having a big party. Look at the drawings and write what each person has to do to get ready for the party. Follow the model.

Modelo Maricarmen: *Tiene que lavarse el pelo*.

1. Paquita: ______________________.
2. Daniel: ______________________.
3. Raúl: ______________________.
4. Rafaelito: ______________________.
5. Frida: ______________________.
6. Amelia: ______________________.
7. José: ______________________.
8. Diego: ______________________.

Realidades 2

Capítulo 2A

Nombre ______________________ Hora ________

Fecha ______________________ Practice Workbook **2A–4**

Más vocabulario

Answer the following questions in complete sentences based on the pictures provided.

1.  ¿Los muchachos están tranquilos o nerviosos?

____

2.  ¿El muchacho se pone gel o agua de colonia?

____

3.  ¿Qué hay que hacer para estar en la obra de teatro?

____

4.  ¿Dónde se pone el maquillaje la muchacha?

____

5.  ¿Está cómodo el muchacho?

____

6.  ¿Qué vas a hacer para prepararte?

____

7.  ¿Qué llevas con los pantalones?

____

8.  ¿Vas a un evento especial?

____

Go Online WEB CODE jdd-0203 PHSchool.com

Realidades 2 | Nombre ______ | Hora ______

Capítulo 2A | Fecha ______ | Practice Workbook **2A–5**

Uno sí, el otro no

Your mother has just gotten home from work, and she wants to know what everyone is up to. Tell her each time that the person she asks about is NOT doing the activity mentioned. Follow the model.

Modelo Paula se baña. ¿Y los niños?
No, los niños no se bañan.

1. Las niñas se acuestan. ¿Y Carla?
______
2. Yo me ducho. ¿Y ustedes?
______
3. Juana se pinta las uñas. ¿Y las otras chicas?
______
4. Lorenzo se cepilla los dientes ahora. ¿Y tú?
______
5. Tú te levantas. ¿Y nosotros?
______
6. Carlos se despierta temprano. ¿Y usted?
______
7. Alicia se corta el pelo. ¿Y yo?
______
8. Nosotros nos vestimos. ¿Y Paco?
______

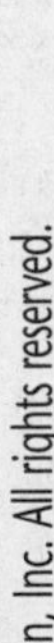

WEB CODE jdd-0205

En el teatro

A. Complete the following sentences with the correct form of the present tense of the verb **ser** or **estar.**

1. Tomás y Raúl ______ actores.
2. Raúl no ______ muy entusiasmado.
3. Tú no ______ muy interesante.
4. Parece que Tomás ______ cómodo.
5. ¿Por qué ______ Ud. tan nervioso? Yo ______ tranquilo.
6. La boda ______ un evento especial para todos.
7. Las joyas ______ aquí, en mi dormitorio.
8. Nosotros ______ de España.

B. Now, write complete sentences from the elements given, using the verb **ser** or **estar** as appropriate.

1. este peine / de Raúl

   ______.
2. el baile / elegante

   ______.
3. yo / en el baño

   ______.
4. nosotros / contentos

   ______.
5. los actores / nerviosos

   ______.
6. la obra / cómica

   ______.

Go Online WEB CODE jdd-0206 PHSchool.com

¡Mamá mía!

A. Rewrite each of these possessive phrases using the long form of possessive adjectives. Follow the model.

Modelo su boda ➜ *la boda suya*

1. mi chaqueta ______
2. nuestras joyas ______
3. tu toalla ______
4. su ropa ______
5. mi cepillo ______
6. tus zapatos ______
7. su sudadera ______
8. nuestros anteojos ______
9. mis botas ______
10. tus calcetines ______

B. Now, create sentences contrasting the elements given. Use the long form of possessive adjectives. Follow the model.

Modelo mi chaqueta / roja ~ tu chaqueta / negra
La chaqueta mía es roja, pero la chaqueta tuya es negra.

1. nuestro libro / aburrido ~ su libro / interesante
______.
2. tu fotografía / bonita ~ nuestra fotografía / fea
______.
3. tu casa / grande ~ mi casa / pequeña
______.
4. mis joyas / de plata ~ sus joyas / de oro
______.
5. nuestros amigos / de México ~ tus amigos / de Costa Rica
______.

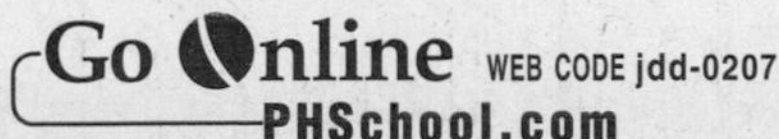
Go Online WEB CODE jdd-0207 PHSchool.com

Repaso

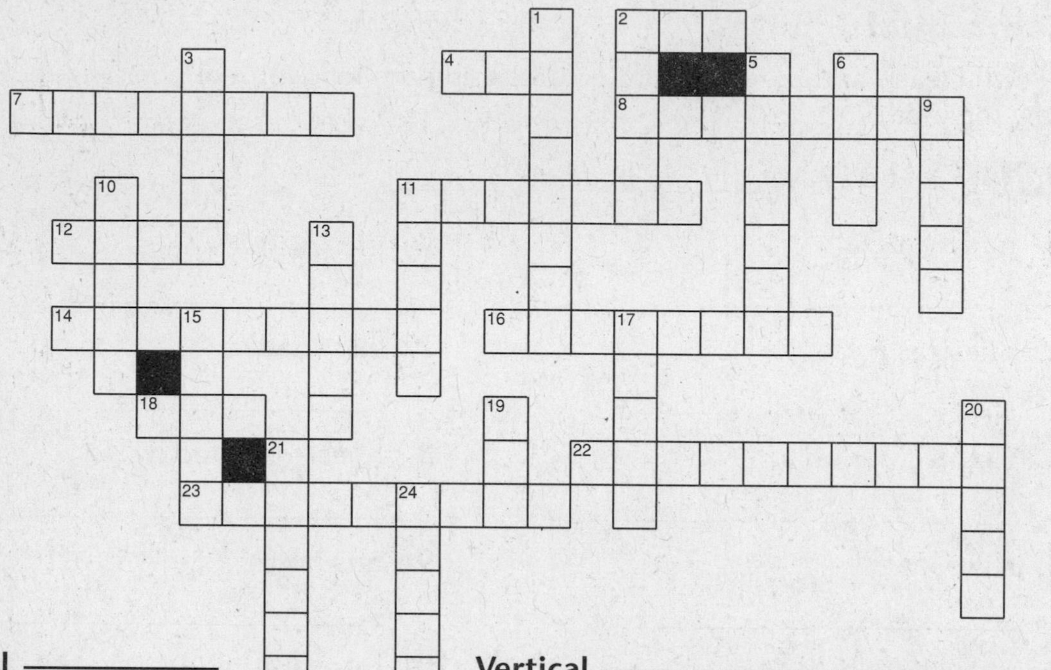

Horizontal

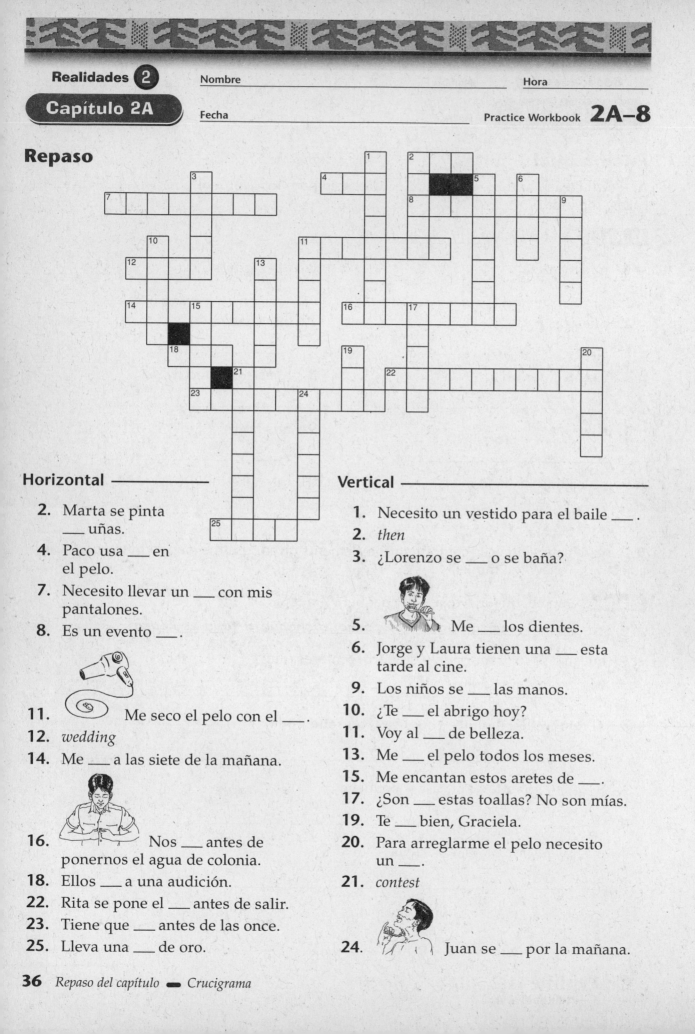

2. Marta se pinta ___ uñas.

4. Paco usa ___ en el pelo.

7. Necesito llevar un ___ con mis pantalones.

8. Es un evento ___.

11. Me seco el pelo con el ___.

12. *wedding*

14. Me ___ a las siete de la mañana.

16. Nos ___ antes de ponernos el agua de colonia.

18. Ellos ___ a una audición.

22. Rita se pone el ___ antes de salir.

23. Tiene que ___ antes de las once.

25. Lleva una ___ de oro.

Vertical

1. Necesito un vestido para el baile ___.

2. *then*

3. ¿Lorenzo se ___ o se baña?

5. Me ___ los dientes.

6. Jorge y Laura tienen una ___ esta tarde al cine.

9. Los niños se ___ las manos.

10. ¿Te ___ el abrigo hoy?

11. Voy al ___ de belleza.

13. Me ___ el pelo todos los meses.

15. Me encantan estos aretes de ___.

17. ¿Son ___ estas toallas? No son mías.

19. Te ___ bien, Graciela.

20. Para arreglarme el pelo necesito un ___.

21. *contest*

24. Juan se ___ por la mañana.

Realidades 2 | Nombre ______ Hora ______

Capítulo 2A | Fecha ______ Practice Workbook **2A–9**

Organizer

I. Vocabulary

Verbs that express one's daily routine | **Words used to describe fixing one's hair**

______ ______

______ ______

______ ______

______ ______

______ ______

Words for events

______ ______

______ ______

II. Grammar

1. To say that you do something to or for yourself, you use a ______ verb.
2. A verb of this type is **lavarse.** Its forms are:

   (yo) ______ (nosotros) ______

   (tú) ______ (vosotros) ______

   (Ud., él, ella) ______ (Uds., ellos, ellas) ______

3. Would you use **ser** or **estar** for each of these purposes? Circle the right verb.

To talk about what a person or thing is or is like	**ser**	**estar**
To talk about how a person feels	**ser**	**estar**
To talk about to whom something belongs	**ser**	**estar**
To talk about what a thing is made of	**ser**	**estar**
To talk about where a person or thing is located	**ser**	**estar**
To talk about where a person or thing is from	**ser**	**estar**

4. The long forms of the possessive adjectives are:

   ______ ______

   ______ ______

   ______

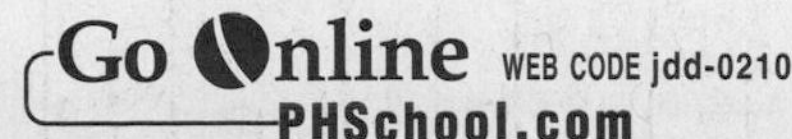

Nombre ______ Hora ______

Fecha ______ Practice Workbook **2B–A**

A ver si recuerdas...

¿Qué es?

A. Complete the sentences by writing the word that corresponds to each picture in the space provided.

1. Jorge compra cosas baratas en la ______________________.

2. Elena no sabe si tiene bastante dinero para ______________ los aretes.

3. Paco y Lidia compran ______________________ para su hermano.

4. Las chicas pasan la tarde en el ______________________.

5. Los señores Vargas buscan cosas para la casa en la tienda de ______________________.

6. A Paco le gustan mucho los ______________________.

7. Sara busca zapatos baratos en la ______________________.

Go Online WEB CODE jdd-0211 PHSchool.com

Realidades 2

Nombre ______ Hora ______

Capítulo 2B

Fecha ______ Practice Workbook **2B–B**

A ver si recuerdas...

¿De qué color es?

A. When unscrambled, each set of letters names a color. Unscramble each one to find out the color of the item mentioned.

1. la cartera ______ o n r a m r
2. el bolso ______ g o n r c
3. las flores ______ a i a s ll m a r
4. la mochila ______ e d v r e
5. los teléfonos ______ i s r s g e
6. la pared ______ a c l n b a

B. Use the cues below to tell what each person is buying at the mall. Follow the model.

Modelo María / 5 / bolso

María compra cinco bolsos ______.

1. Roberto y Felipe / 10 / collar

______.

2. yo / 50 / discos compactos

______.

3. tú / 3 / cartera

______.

4. Uds. / 20 / videojuegos

______.

5. nosotros / 12 / botella de perfume

______.

Nombre ______ Hora ______

Fecha ______ Practice Workbook **2B–1**

¿Qué hacen?

A. Look at the drawings and tell what the people are doing.

1. Ricardo paga en la ______.
2. Cristina ______ un vestido.
3. Leonor quiere pagar con ______.
4. Juan Carlos no encuentra su ______.
5. Emilio paga la camiseta con ______.

B. Tell about Lucero's shopping spree in the department store by writing in the missing words from the word bank.

tarjeta	**cheque**	**estilos**	**efectivo**	**gasté**

1. El almacén tiene ropa de varios ______.
2. Yo ______ mucho dinero.
3. Pagué con mi ______ de crédito.
4. También tenía un ______ de viajero de mi viaje a San Antonio.
5. Nunca pago con dinero en ______.

Go Online
WEB CODE jdd-0212
PHSchool.com

Realidades 2 Nombre ______________ Hora ______

Capítulo 2B Fecha ______________ Practice Workbook **2B–2**

¿Qué dices?

A. Decide whether each pair of words is a synonym or an antonym. Circle the correct one.

1.	la entrada	la salida	**sinónimo**	**antónimo**
2.	el número	la talla	**sinónimo**	**antónimo**
3.	color claro	color oscuro	**sinónimo**	**antónimo**
4.	precio bajo	precio alto	**sinónimo**	**antónimo**
5.	liquidación	ganga	**sinónimo**	**antónimo**

B. Tell what Paulina and Rosaura are saying about shopping in the department store by filling in the missing letters.

PAULINA: Ahora me p_ _ _ _ _ _ esta falda negra. ¿Qué te _ _ r _ c _ ? ¿Me queda bien?

ROSAURA: Yo prefiero los colores _ i _ _ _. ¿No te gusta _ q _ e _ _ _ falda roja?

PAULINA: Bueno, voy a probarme las dos. Las _ _ r c _ _ son buenas.

ROSAURA: ¿Y sabes que hay un descuento del 25 por ciento?

PAULINA: Con estos p _ _ _ _ _ _ s tan bajos, puedo comprar blusas y jeans también.

ROSAURA: De acuerdo. No son tan _ x a _ _ _ a _ _ _ como en otras tiendas.

PAULINA: Y yo voy a buscar un abrigo. Me encanta el _ s _ _ _ o de aquel abrigo gris.

ROSAURA: Sí, está muy de _ _ d _. Vamos a ver si tienen en talla m _ _ _ _ n _.

PAULINA: El _ _ _ _ _ _ _ o anuncia un descuento del 50 por ciento. ¡Qué _ _ n _ _!

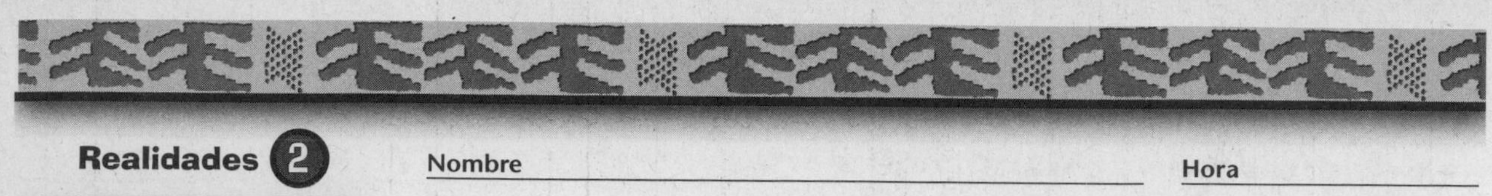

Nombre ____________________ Hora __________

Fecha ____________________ Practice Workbook **2B–3**

¿Qué quieres?

Answer the following questions using the items pictured as clues. Follow the model.

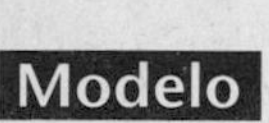

Modelo  ¿Esa blusa es de color claro? *No, la blusa es de color oscuro*.

1. ¿De qué está hecho el suéter? ____________________.

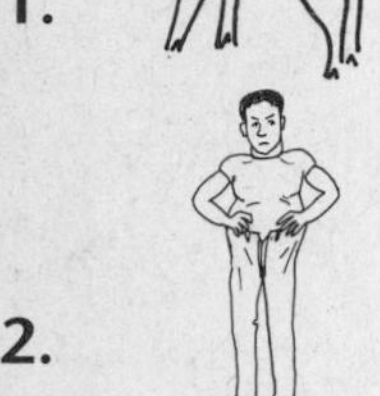

2. ¿Cómo te quedan los pantalones? ____________________.

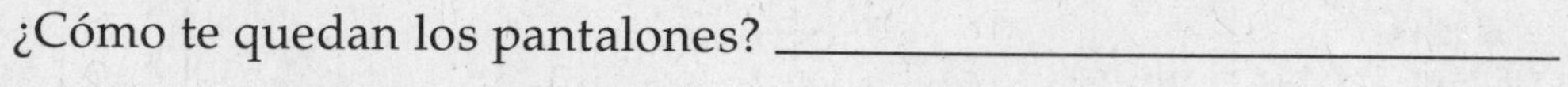

3. ¿Cómo vas a pagar por esto? ____________________.

4. ¿En dónde vas a pagar? ____________________.

5. ¿Adónde vas para gastar tu dinero? ____________________.

6. ¿Cuál talla te queda mejor? ____________________.

7. ¿Qué anuncia el letrero? ____________________.

8. ¿Qué usas para salir? ____________________.

En el centro comercial

Tatiana and Mariana are in the mall for the many clearance sales going on today. Read their conversation and answer the questions that follow.

MARIANA: Mira, aquí hay liquidación de camisetas de colores vivos.
TATIANA: Viene el invierno. Yo quiero ropa más grande de colores oscuros.
MARIANA: Entonces no vas a encontrar ropa en liquidación. Tampoco vas a encontrar ropa de moda.
TATIANA: Está bien. No tiene que ser una ganga, sólo un precio no demasiado exagerado.
MARIANA: ¿Te gusta esta blusa? Es de algodón. Y también es de una marca popular.
TATIANA: Sí. También me gusta aquella falda. ¿Sabes de qué está hecha?
MARIANA: Parece de cuero.
TATIANA: En realidad no me importa. Se ve bien con la blusa. Me las voy a probar.

MARIANA: ¿Cómo te quedan?
TATIANA: Bastante bien. La blusa está un poco floja y la falda está un poco apretada.
MARIANA: Te ves muy bien. ¿Quieres buscar algo más?
TATIANA: ¿Por qué no miramos esas camisetas en liquidación?
MARIANA: ¡Vamos!

1. ¿Qué busca Tatiana?

____.

2. En realidad, ¿quiere una ganga Tatiana? ¿Te parece que el precio le importa más a Mariana? ¿Por qué?

____
____
____.

3. ¿Por qué le gusta la falda a Tatiana? ¿A ella le importa la tela?

____
____.

4. ¿Cómo le queda la ropa a Tatiana?

____.

5. En tu opinión, ¿Tatiana va a comprar la falda y la blusa? ¿Por qué?

____
____
____.

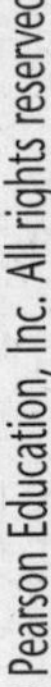

Nombre ______________________ Hora ______

Fecha ______________________ Practice Workbook **2B–5**

¿Qué hicieron?

A. Alicia and her friends went shopping yesterday. Complete the following sentences to tell what they saw and bought. Use the preterite of the verbs given. Follow the model.

Modelo Alicia y sus amigos / decidir
Alicia y sus amigos decidieron ir de compras.

1. Alicia y sus amigos / llegar
   ______________________ al mercado.
2. Tú / ver
   ______________________ una liquidación.
3. Ellos / entrar
   ______________________ en la tienda.
4. Alicia / recibir
   ______________________ un descuento.
5. La tienda / anunciar
   ______________________ la ganga del siglo.
6. Jorge / escoger
   ______________________ unos pantalones.
7. Marta y Felisa / encontrar
   ______________________ faldas y zapatos.
8. Todos / gastar
   ______________________ mucho dinero.

B. Alfredo describes what he did yesterday. Supply the correct **yo** form of the verbs in parentheses to complete his narration.

1. (llegar) ______________ a la escuela a las ocho menos cuarto.
2. (navegar) En la sala de computadoras ______________ en la Red.
3. (tocar) ______________ en la orquesta de la escuela.
4. (almorzar) ______________ con mis amigos.
5. (buscar) ______________ mi libro de química.
6. (empezar) ______________ a estudiar para el examen.

Go Online WEB CODE jdd-0214
PHSchool.com

Aquél es mío

A. Write sentences to tell who the things over there belong to.

Modelo llavero/yo *Aquel llavero es mío*.

1. cupones de regalo/él ____________.
2. tarjeta de crédito/nosotros ____________.
3. cheques personales/tú ____________.
4. bolso/ella ____________.
5. cartera/yo ____________.
6. joyas/ellas ____________.

B. Look at the drawings below. Answer the questions based on the article of clothing that is indicated. Follow the model.

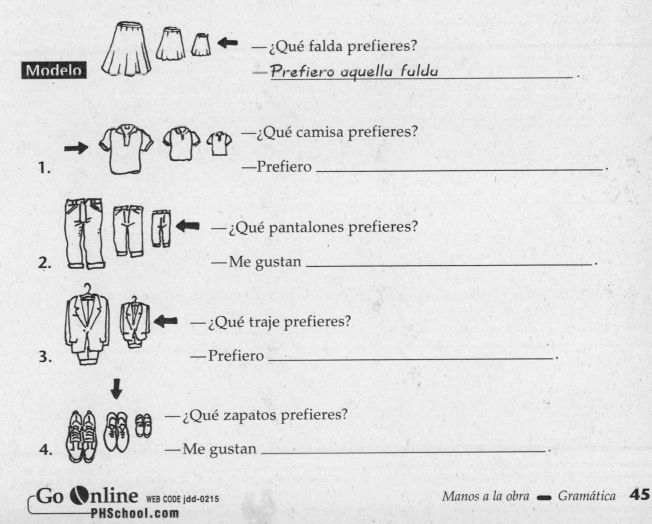

Modelo 
—¿Qué falda prefieres?
—*Prefiero aquella falda*.

1. —¿Qué camisa prefieres?
—Prefiero ____________.

2. —¿Qué pantalones prefieres?
—Me gustan ____________.

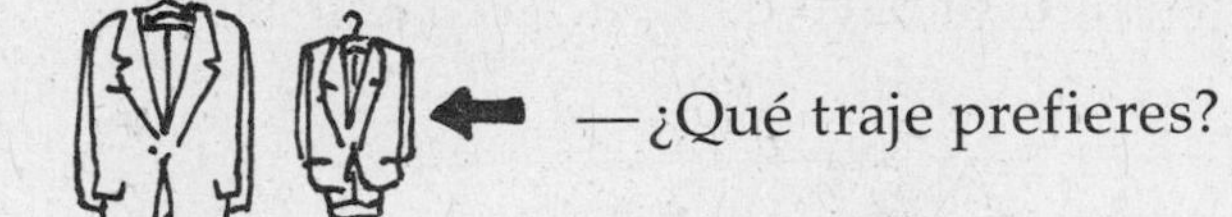

3. —¿Qué traje prefieres?
—Prefiero ____________.

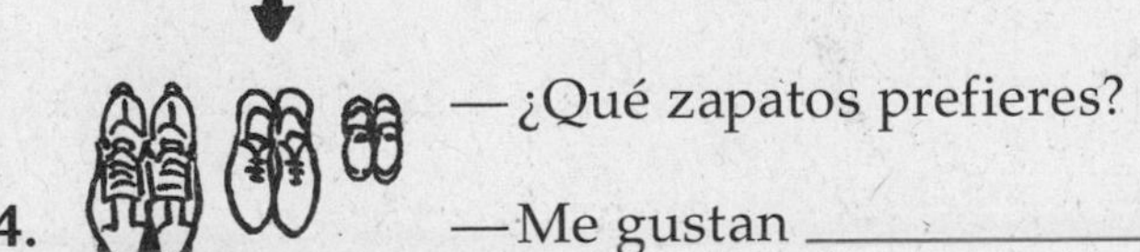

4. —¿Qué zapatos prefieres?
—Me gustan ____________.

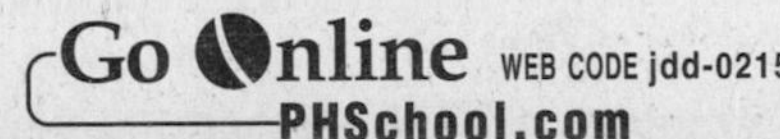

Uno de ésos

Answer each of the following questions in a complete sentence. Use the correct preterite form of the verb and the underlined noun to answer the questions. Follow the model.

Modelo ¿Compraste una camisa de algodón o <u>una camisa de lana</u>?

Compré una de lana ______________________________.

1. ¿Compraron ustedes <u>el cinturón de tela</u> o el cinturón de cuero?

   ______________________________.

2. ¿Encontraste una blusa blanca o <u>una blusa azul</u>?

   ______________________________.

3. ¿Se probó Juana unos pantalones de color claro o <u>unos pantalones de color oscuro</u>?

   ______________________________.

4. ¿Escogiste <u>un bolso caro</u> o un bolso barato?

   ______________________________.

5. ¿Vieron ustedes <u>muchos estilos nuevos</u> o pocos estilos nuevos?

   ______________________________.

6. ¿Buscaste una gorra roja o <u>una gorra negra</u>?

   ______________________________.

7. ¿Escribieron ustedes unas composiciones largas o <u>unas composiciones cortas</u>?

   ______________________________.

8. ¿Te gustó más <u>el disco compacto de Laura</u> o el disco compacto de Carmen?

   ______________________________.

Go Online WEB CODE jdd-0216 PHSchool.com

Repaso

Horizontal

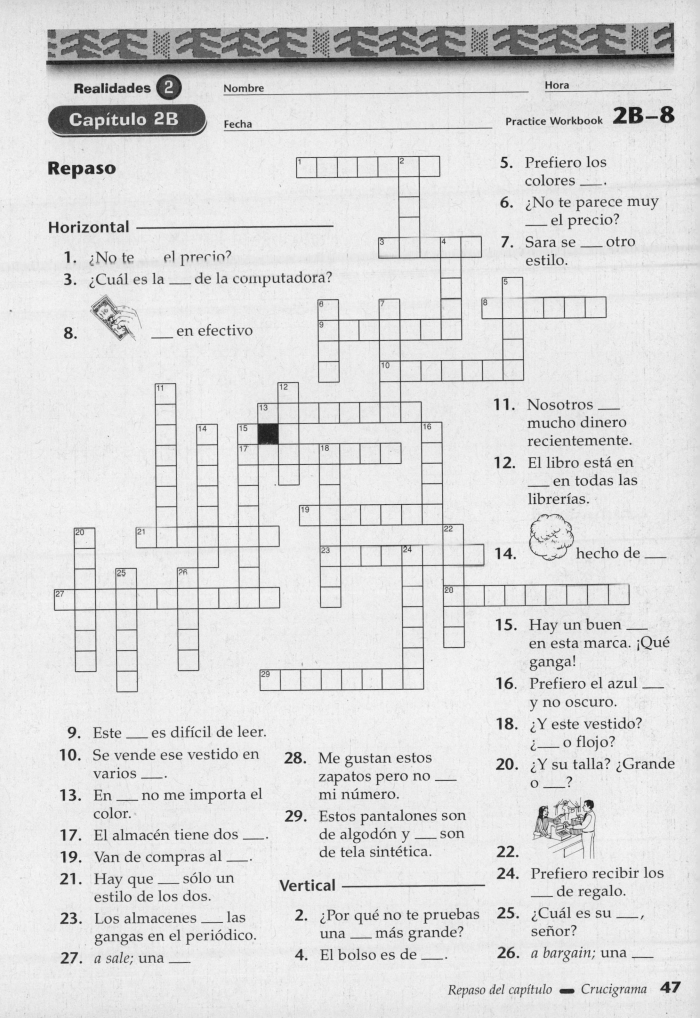

1. ¿No te ___ el precio?
3. ¿Cuál es la ___ de la computadora?
5. Prefiero los colores ___.
6. ¿No te parece muy ___ el precio?
7. Sara se ___ otro estilo.
8. ___ en efectivo
9. Este ___ es difícil de leer.
10. Se vende ese vestido en varios ___.
13. En ___ no me importa el color.
17. El almacén tiene dos ___.
19. Van de compras al ___.
21. Hay que ___ sólo un estilo de los dos.
23. Los almacenes ___ las gangas en el periódico.
27. *a sale;* una ___
28. Me gustan estos zapatos pero no ___ mi número.
29. Estos pantalones son de algodón y ___ son de tela sintética.

Vertical

2. ¿Por qué no te pruebas una ___ más grande?
4. El bolso es de ___.
11. Nosotros ___ mucho dinero recientemente.
12. El libro está en ___ en todas las librerías.
14. ___ hecho de ___
15. Hay un buen ___ en esta marca. ¡Qué ganga!
16. Prefiero el azul ___ y no oscuro.
18. ¿Y este vestido? ¿___ o flojo?
20. ¿Y su talla? ¿Grande o ___?
22. 
24. Prefiero recibir los ___ de regalo.
25. ¿Cuál es su ___, señor?
26. *a bargain;* una ___

Organizer

I. Vocabulary

Words that describe fabrics

____

____

____

____

____

Words used to describe ways of paying

____

____

____

____

____

Words for fashion and style

_______________ _______________

_______________ _______________

II. Grammar

1. Give the preterite forms of these verbs.

mirar	**comer**	**escribir**

2. Fill in the following chart with the forms of **aquel.**

	singular	**plural**
masculine		
feminine		

3. When comparing two similar things you can avoid repetition by using an _______________ as a noun.

Realidades 2 | Nombre ______________________ | Hora ______

Capítulo 3A | Fecha ______________________ | Practice Workbook **3A–A**

A ver si recuerdas...

Vamos a hacer los quehaceres

Look at the drawings and tell what chores people are doing.

1. María ______________________________.

2. Ignacio ______________________________.

3. Gregorio ______________________________.

4. Rebeca ______________________________ al perro.

5. Sandra ______________________________.

6. Raquel ______________________________.

7. Antonio y Sergio ______________________________.

8. Carmen ______________________________.

9. Felipe y Cristina ______________________________.

10. Ana ______________________________.

A ver si recuerdas...

¿A qué hora?

Look at the schedule below of the new high-speed train and answer the questions that follow in complete sentences. Follow the model.

Salir de	Llegar a	Duración
Boston	Washington, D.C.	4 horas
Nueva York	Montreal	5 horas
Philadelphia	Miami	7 horas
Baltimore	Atlanta	6 horas

Modelo Si el tren llega a Montreal a las nueve de la noche, ¿a qué hora salió de Nueva York?

El tren salió de Nueva York a las cuatro de la tarde.

1. Si el tren llega a Miami a las tres de la tarde, ¿a qué hora salió de Philadelphia?

   ______________________________.

2. Si el tren salió de Boston a las cinco de la tarde, ¿a qué hora llega a Washington, D.C.?

   ______________________________.

3. Si el tren llega a Atlanta a las nueve de la mañana, ¿a qué hora salió de Baltimore?

   ______________________________.

4. Un tren salió de Boston a la una y media de la tarde. ¿A qué hora va a llegar a Washington?

   ______________________________.

5. El tren va a llegar a Miami a las once y cuarto de la noche. ¿A qué hora salió de Philadelphia?

   ______________________________.

6. Si el tren salió de Boston a las once de la noche, ¿a qué hora llega a Washington, D.C.?

   ______________________________.

7. El tren va a llegar a Montreal a las ocho y media de la noche. ¿A qué hora salió de Nueva York?

   ______________________________.

Go Online WEB CODE jdd-0301
PHSchool.com

Pasando por el centro

A. You are giving a tour of your hometown to Luis, the exchange student from Caracas. Using the art to help you, tell him where each building is.

1. Aquí está ______________________.
2. Y allí está ______________________.
3. A la izquierda queda ______________________.
4. Y a la derecha queda ______________________.
5. Enfrente de esto queda ______________________.
6. Al fin de la calle está ______________________.

B. You and Luis decide to go into the sports store, and you are thinking about buying something. Fill in the blanks below to complete your conversation with Luis.

TÚ: Quiero jugar al hockey este año.

LUIS: Tienes que buscar el ______________ deportivo apropiado. No puedes jugar si no tienes las cosas que necesitas.

TÚ: Sí, primero necesito unos ______________ .

LUIS: De acuerdo. Me encanta patinar.

TÚ: En la primavera quiero también jugar al golf.

LUIS: Quizás necesitas un ______________ de golf nuevo.

TÚ: ¡Cómo no! Y si no juego al golf, puedo jugar al tenis.

LUIS: Y no puedes jugar al tenis sin ______________ . Hay varias aquí para todos los deportes.

TÚ: ¿Quieres jugar al tenis conmigo? Puedo comprarte una ______________ de tenis.

LUIS: No, gracias, ya la tengo.

Un día de quehaceres

A. Tell what Lucas is doing by filling in the missing words from the word bank. You will not use all of the words from the bank. NOTE: the words in the bank are scrambled.

ócsa	**satpa**	**reab**	**ploceil**	**tisdtean**
robcra	**lovederv**	**ózubn**	**losles**	**qecuhe**
sica	**reraci**	**cúmaph**	**aacrt**	**édmoci**

1. Lucas va al supermercado para comprar el ____________________ para lavarse el pelo.
2. Luego, va a la biblioteca para ____________________ el libro que leyó ayer.
3. Lo ____________________ la semana pasada de la biblioteca y le gustó mucho.
4. El correo se ____________________ a las nueve, entonces va al consultorio primero.
5. En el consultorio habla con el ____________________ porque le duele el estómago.
6. En el correo, Lucas tiene que comprar unos ____________________.
7. Los necesita para enviar una ____________________ a su abuelo.
8. Después, va a echarla en el ____________________.
9. Tiene que ir al banco después porque se ____________________ a las cuatro.
10. En el banco va a ____________________ su ____________________ del trabajo.
11. Al fin del día compra un ____________________ de dientes porque tiene que ir al consultorio de la ____________________ la semana que viene.
12. Ahora, sólo le falta la ____________________ dental para cepillarse los dientes.

Go Online WEB CODE jdd-0302 PHSchool.com

A ver qué hace la gente

Answer the questions, using the drawings as clues. Follow the model.

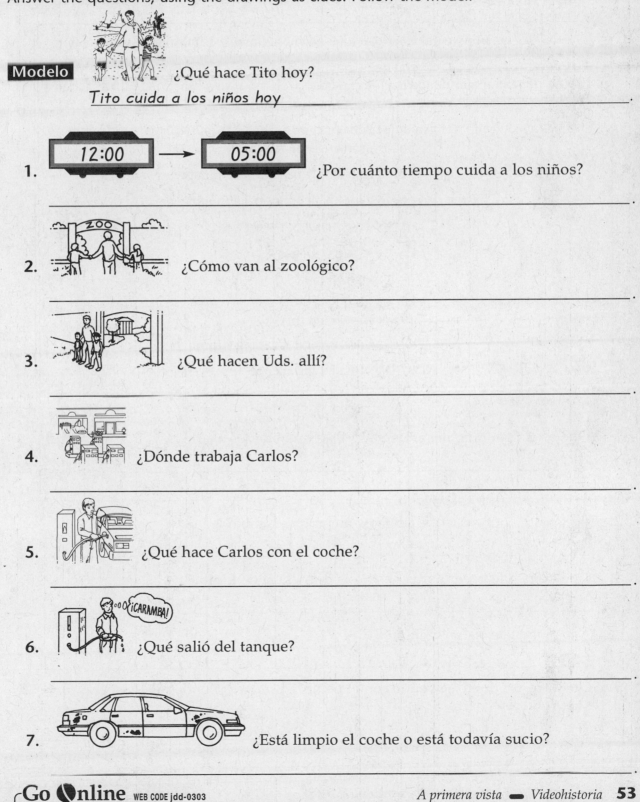

Modelo ¿Qué hace Tito hoy?

Tito cuida a los niños hoy.

1. ¿Por cuánto tiempo cuida a los niños?

____.

2. ¿Cómo van al zoológico?

____.

3. ¿Qué hacen Uds. allí?

____.

4. ¿Dónde trabaja Carlos?

____.

5. ¿Qué hace Carlos con el coche?

____.

6. ¿Qué salió del tanque?

____.

7. ¿Está limpio el coche o está todavía sucio?

____.

Nombre ______________________ Hora __________

Fecha ______________________ Practice Workbook **3A–4**

El jabón perfecto

Read the following advertisement and answer the questions based on what you read.

¿Quiere Ud. un jabón de alta calidad[1] que no cuesta tanto? **Limba** debe ser su jabón.

Hay otros jabones que dicen que tienen la fórmula más poderosa[2] pero la marca **Limba** tiene la mejor de todas. Sólo hay que probarlo y va a saber que no hay jabón mejor que **Limba**.

Los médicos dicen: "La gente que se lava con **Limba** es la más contenta y tiene muy pocos problemas de la piel[3]."

Limba es lo mejor en higiene, salud y belleza para hombres y mujeres.

Debe comprarlo ahora para conocer la diferencia.

También se puede comprar Champú **Limba**.

De venta en farmacias.

[1]*quality* [2]*powerful* [3]*skin*

1. ¿Qué es el producto del anuncio? ¿Para qué puedes usarlo?

____

____

2. Según este anuncio, ¿qué jabón es mejor que **Limba**?

____

3. ¿Qué tiene que hacer para conocer la diferencia de **Limba**?

____

4. ¿A los médicos les gusta **Limba**?

____

5. ¿Qué otro producto se vende con el nombre **Limba**? ¿Dónde puedes comprar este producto?

____

____

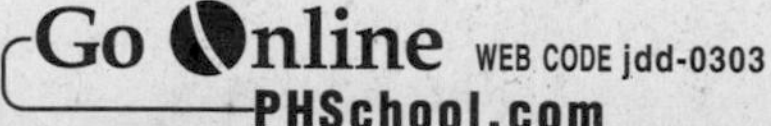

Nombre ______ Hora ______

Fecha ______ Practice Workbook **3A–5**

Tengo que hacerlo

Complete the following exchanges about errands people have to run today with the missing direct object pronouns. Follow the model.

Modelo —¿Ayudaron ustedes a sus amigas con la tarea?
—Sí, ___las___ ayudamos después de la clase.

1. —¿Tienes la pasta dental?
   —No hay. No ______________ compré.
2. —¿Vas a enviar la carta?
   —Sí, ______________ eché al buzón hace una hora.
3. —¿Tienes que devolver los libros?
   —No, ______________ saqué ayer.
4. —¿Necesitas comprarte una raqueta de tenis?
   —No, ya ______________ tengo.
5. —Necesito más champú.
   —Puedo comprar______________ en el supermercado.
6. —¿A qué hora se cierra el banco? Necesito cobrar unos cheques.
   —Se cierra a las cinco. ______________ puedes cobrar ahora.
7. —¿Hay gasolina en el tanque?
   —Sí, ______________ llenamos hoy por la mañana.
8. —¿Tienes sellos?
   —Sí, ______________ compré hoy por la mañana.

Un día...

A. Tell where these people went by completing each sentence with the correct preterite form of the verb **ir**. Follow the model.

Modelo Teresa ___fue___ a la biblioteca.

1. Yo __________ al banco.
2. Ud. __________ a la farmacia.
3. Mis amigos y yo __________ al supermercado.
4. ¿Tú __________ al correo?
5. Ramón y Manolo __________ a la estación de servicio.
6. Mis padres __________ a casa.
7. Javier __________ a la tienda de equipo deportivo.

B. Tell what each of these things was like. Use the preterite of the verb **ser** and the correct form of the adjective given. Follow the model.

Modelo 

/ largo ___La obra fue larga___.

1. 207 / interesante __________.
2.  / difícil __________.
3.  / emocionante __________.
4.  / fantástico __________.
5.  / divertido __________.

Go Online WEB CODE jdd-0305 PHSchool.com

Conversaciones

A. Complete the following conversation between Rosa and her friends with the missing forms of the verbs **estar, poder,** and **tener** in the preterite.

AMIGOS: Ayer fuimos a la tienda de equipo deportivo. Nosotros (1) ________ en la tienda por una hora.

ROSA: ¿(2) ________ encontrar las camisetas?

AMIGOS: No, allí no. (3) ________ que ir a otra tienda. Allí las (4) ________ comprar.

B. Complete the following conversation between Tomás and Clara with the missing preterite forms of the verbs **estar, hacer, poder,** and **tener.**

TOMÁS: ¿Cuántas horas pasaste en la biblioteca ayer?

CLARA: (1) ________ allí cuatro horas por la tarde.

TOMÁS: ¿(2) ________ terminar tu informe?

CLARA: No, no lo (3) ________ terminar.

TOMÁS: ¿Qué (4) ________ entonces?

CLARA: (5) ________ que volver por la noche.

TOMÁS: ¿Fuiste sola?

CLARA: Sí. Nadie (6) ________ ir conmigo.

Repaso

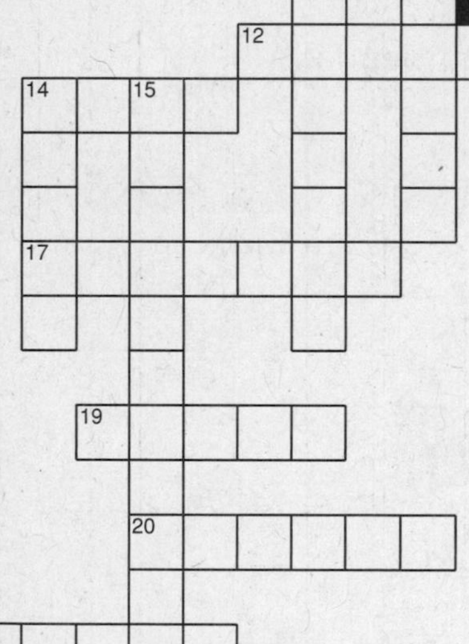

Horizontal

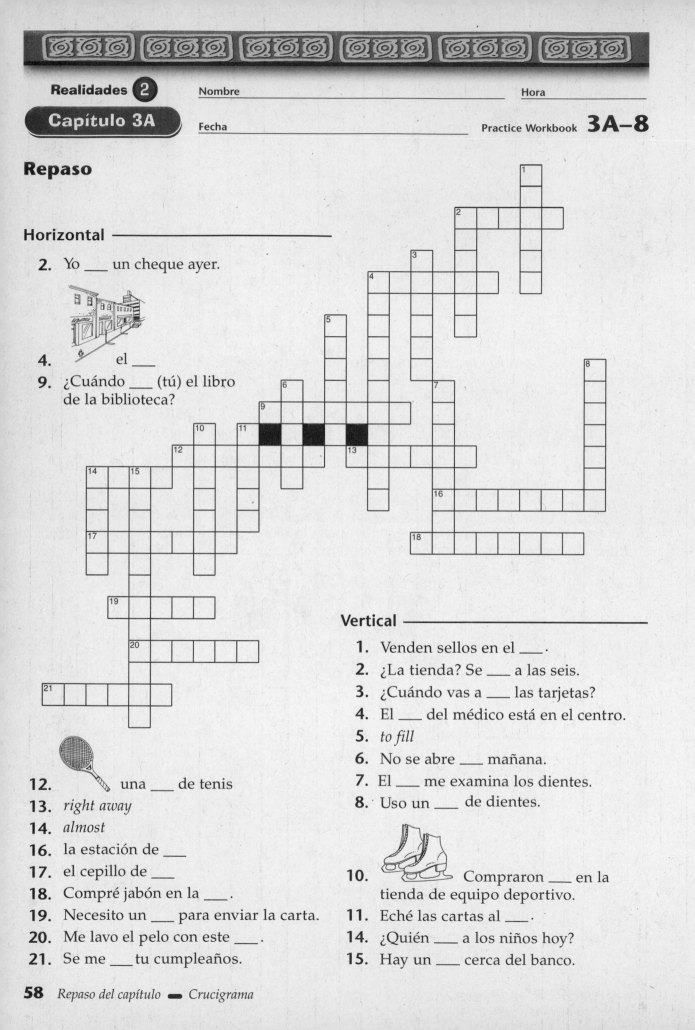

2. Yo ___ un cheque ayer.

4. el ___
9. ¿Cuándo ___ (tú) el libro de la biblioteca?
12. una ___ de tenis
13. *right away*
14. *almost*
16. la estación de ___
17. el cepillo de ___
18. Compré jabón en la ___.
19. Necesito un ___ para enviar la carta.
20. Me lavo el pelo con este ___.
21. Se me ___ tu cumpleaños.

Vertical

1. Venden sellos en el ___.
2. ¿La tienda? Se ___ a las seis.
3. ¿Cuándo vas a ___ las tarjetas?
4. El ___ del médico está en el centro.
5. *to fill*
6. No se abre ___ mañana.
7. El ___ me examina los dientes.
8. Uso un ___ de dientes.

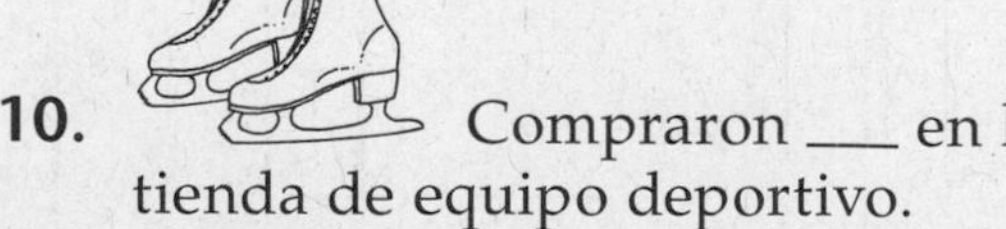

10. Compraron ___ en la tienda de equipo deportivo.
11. Eché las cartas al ___.
14. ¿Quién ___ a los niños hoy?
15. Hay un ___ cerca del banco.

Organizer

I. Vocabulary

Words to talk about mail

____
____
____
____
____

Items found in a sporting goods store

____
____
____
____
____

Items bought in a drugstore

____
____
____
____

Places in a community

____
____
____
____

II. Grammar

1. List the four direct object pronouns that correspond to *him, her, it,* and *them.*

   ________, ________, ________, ________

2. Give the preterite forms of these verbs.

ir y ser		estar	
________	________	________	________
________	________	________	________
________	________	________	________

poder		mirar	
________	________	________	________
________	________	________	________
________	________	________	________

Nombre ______________________ Hora ______________

Fecha ______________________ Practice Workbook **3B–A**

A ver si recuerdas...

¿Dónde está?

Fill in the blanks with the location of each item as pictured. Follow the model.

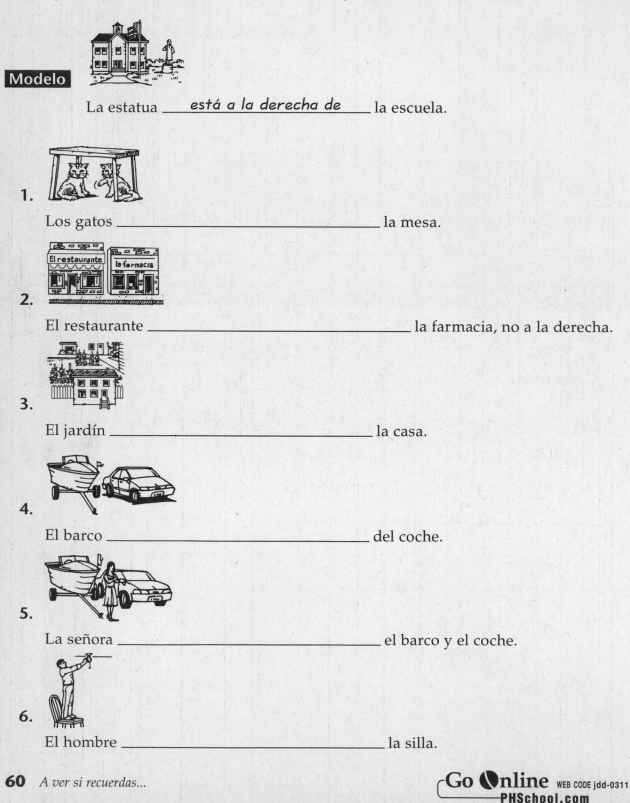

Modelo

La estatua *está a la derecha de* la escuela.

1. Los gatos ______________________ la mesa.

2. El restaurante ______________________ la farmacia, no a la derecha.

3. El jardín ______________________ la casa.

4. El barco ______________________ del coche.

5. La señora ______________________ el barco y el coche.

6. El hombre ______________________ la silla.

Realidades 2 | Nombre ______ | Hora ______

Capítulo 3B | Fecha ______ | Practice Workbook **3B–B**

A ver si recuerdas...

¿Cómo viajan?

A. Look at the drawings and tell what form of transportation people are using.

1. La familia Vargas viaja en ______________.
2. Emilia y Leticia toman el ______________.
3. Los niños suben al ______________ para ir a la escuela.
4. Mirian y Miguel toman ______________.
5. La familia Castillo hace un viaje en ______________.
6. A Paco y a Luz María les gusta viajar en ______________.

B. Pedro's mother thinks she already knows the answers to her questions, but she's wrong. Write Pedro's response to each question. Follow the model.

Modelo Pedro, ¿qué haces? ¿La tarea? (ejercicio)
No, hago ejercicio.

1. Pedro, ¿cuándo sales? ¿A las ocho? (a las nueve)
______________.
2. Pedro, ¿qué traes a casa de Amelia? ¿Flores? (dulces)
______________.
3. Pedro, ¿qué dices? ¿Que es mejor? (que es peor)
______________.
4. Pedro, ¿cuándo vienes? ¿Hoy? (mañana)
______________.
5. Pedro, ¿qué tienes? ¿Un coche? (una bicicleta)
______________.

¿Cómo se llega?

Describe the truck's journey by filling in the missing words in the sentences below. Use the picture as a guide.

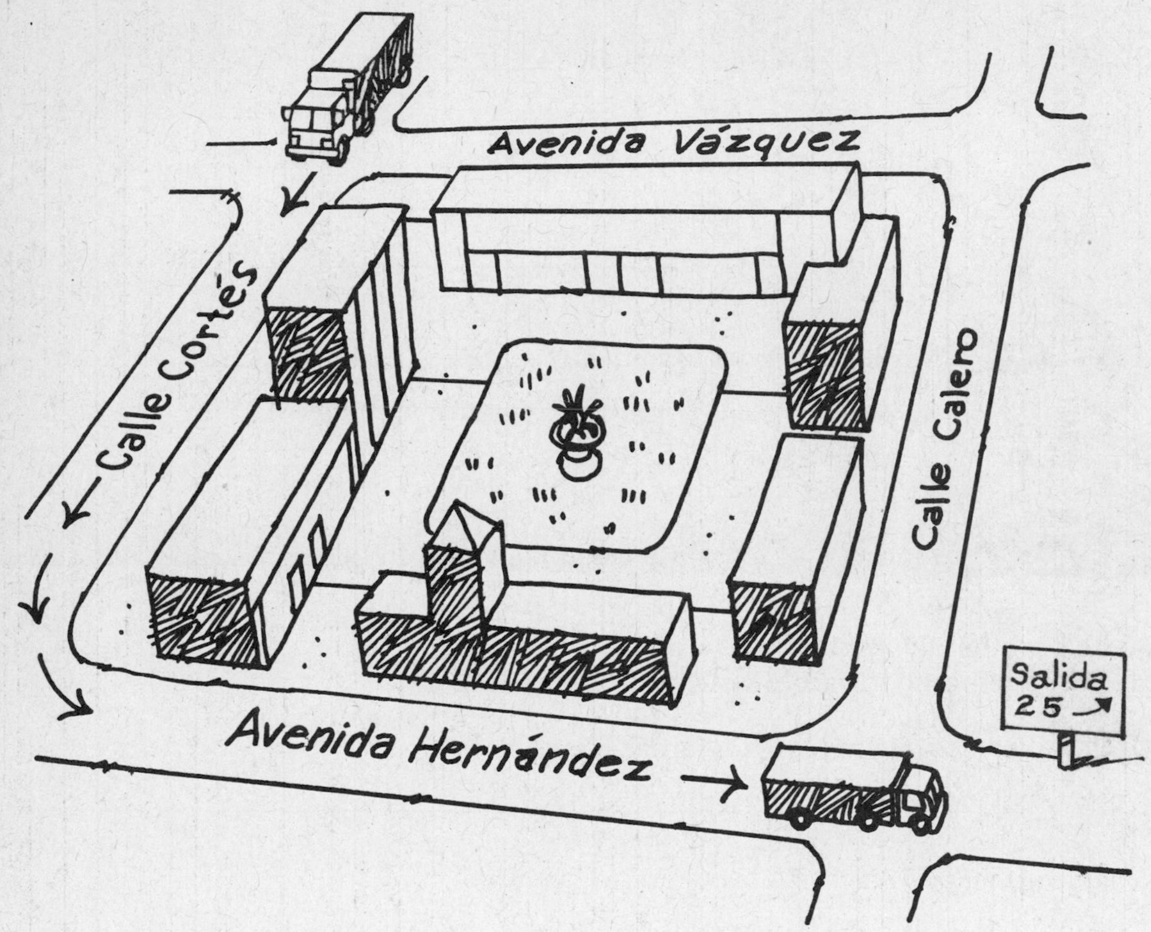

1. El ____________________ está en la Calle Cortés.
2. ____________________ por dos cuadras.
3. ____________________ en la ____________________ de la Calle Cortés y la Avenida Hernández.
4. Este cruce es ____________________ entonces el conductor tiene cuidado.
5. No para en la ____________________ que está a la izquierda.
6. ____________________ derecho en la Avenida Hernández hasta la Calle Calero.
7. ____________________ la Calle Calero hasta llegar a la ____________________.

WEB CODE jdd-0312

¿Qué hacen?

Look at the drawings and tell what the people are doing.

1. El policía le pone ______________________________.

2. Los peatones cruzan la calle en ______________________________.

3. Donaldo y María pasan por ______________________________.

4. El coche dobla en ______________________________.

5. Victoria está al lado de ______________________________.

6. Teresa espera al lado de ______________________________.

7. Hay muchos ______________________________ en la calle.

8. Luis y Carmen esperan en ______________________________.

Mi diccionario

A. Write the appropriate word for each definition.

1. ______________ Personas que van a pie
2. ______________ Persona que maneja el coche
3. ______________ Tren que va debajo de las calles de la ciudad
4. ______________ Persona que pone una multa
5. ______________ Los coches, camiones y autobuses que pasan por las calles de la ciudad
6. ______________ El opuesto (*opposite*) de rápidamente
7. ______________ Más o menos
8. ______________ Difícil de entender o comprender

B. Fill in the missing words according to the illustrations.

1. Las dos muchachas toman ______________.

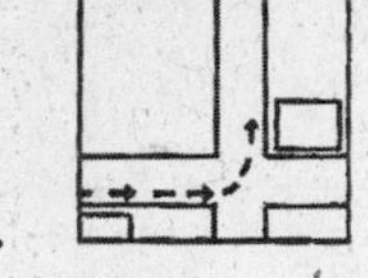

2. Hay que ______________ a la derecha.

3. El coche tiene que ______________.

4. Jaime ______________ a su novia cerca de la estatua.

5. Para llegar al banco hay que cruzar ______________.

Go Online WEB CODE jdd-0313
PHSchool.com

Andando por la ciudad

Complete the following sentences with the appropriate missing words.

1. —A veces doblo a la derecha donde se prohíbe doblar y...

   —¿Qué pasa? ¿El policía te pone una ______________?

2. —¿Puedes hablar conmigo ahora?

   —Lo siento, pero no tengo tiempo. Tengo mucha ______________ ahora.

3. —Allí está el banco. ¿Puedes ______________ el coche? Tengo que sacar algún dinero.

   —Ah, pues yo también. Voy a aparcar aquí.

4. —¿De veras sabes dónde queda el bazar, Francisco?

   —Sí, estoy ______________ de que está a siete cuadras de aquí.

5. —¿El restaurante queda lejos?

   —No, no tan lejos. Queda ______________ a veinte o veinticinco minutos de mi casa.

6. —Creo que es mejor ir a pie.

   —Sí, vamos a ______________ el coche en el garaje y caminar.

7. —¿Por qué no tomamos el metro?

   —______________. Buena idea. En metro llegamos más rápidamente.

8. —Dobla primero a la izquierda, después a la derecha, después a la izquierda otra vez y luego...

   —Esto es muy ______________. ¡Se me olvida ya!

Conversaciones

Complete the following exchanges with the missing direct object pronouns. Follow the model.

Modelo —¿No ves que estoy aquí?

—No, no ___*te*___ veo.

1. —No creo que José entendió lo que dijiste.

   —No sé. Normalmente él __________ entiende bien.

2. —¿Ya tienes el permiso de manejar?

   —Sí, ya __________ tengo.

3. —Laura, Elena, ¿quieren ustedes venir a mi fiesta esta noche?

   —Sí, claro. __________ invitaste la semana pasada.

4. —Termino el trabajo a las seis. Luego voy a tu casa.

   —Bueno, __________ espero en mi casa a las seis y media.

5. —¿Tienen ustedes problemas con la tarea?

   —Sí, puedes ayudar__________ esta noche?

6. —¿Sabes que vamos a jugar al fútbol el sábado?

   —Sí, Martín __________ habló por teléfono anoche.

7. —José y yo tenemos que ir al estadio pero no tenemos coche.

   —No te preocupes, Luis. Creo que Manolo __________ puede llevar.

8. —¿__________ conoces a mí? Me llamo Julio.

   —No, no __________ conozco.

Go Online WEB CODE jdd-0314
PHSchool.com

Tienes que hacer esto

A. Complete the following sentences with the affirmative **tú** commands of the verbs in parentheses.

1. (ser) ________________ bueno, Joselito.
2. (poner) ________________ los libros en el carro.
3. (venir) ________________ conmigo a la playa.
4. (ir) ________________ a pie. Con el tráfico que hay, es más rápido.
5. (decir) ________________ la verdad.
6. (hacer) ________________ la tarea antes de llamar a tu novia.
7. (salir) ________________ de aquí inmediatamente.
8. (tener) ________________ cuidado. Esta carretera es muy peligrosa.

B. Rewrite the following sentences, replacing the noun in italics with the appropriate direct object pronoun. Follow the model.

Modelo Ayuda a *Marta.* Ayúdala.

1. Haz *la tarea.* ________________.
2. Espera a *tus amigos* al lado de la estatua. ________________.
3. Deja *el coche* en el garaje. ________________.
4. Di *la verdad.* ________________.
5. Pon *el mapa* en la mesa. ________________.
6. Escucha *estas canciones.* ________________.

Ahora mismo

Say what the following people are doing now that is different from what they normally do. Follow the model.

Modelo Generalmente, Juan maneja despacio.
Ahora *está manejando* rápido.

1. Normalmente, Diego dice mentiras.
   Ahora ______________ la verdad.
2. Cada día los peatones no siguen por aquella avenida.
   Hoy sí ______________ por aquella avenida.
3. Generalmente, repetimos las direcciones cuando las recibimos.
   Ahora no ______________ nada.
4. En un día normal, los peatones se visten de amarillo.
   Hoy día los peatones ______________ de anaranjado.
5. Normalmente, Uds. leen el manual de manejar.
   Ahora Uds. no ______________ el manual.
6. Liliana cruza la calle con su mamá todos los días.
   Pero ahora no ______________ la calle porque está sola.
7. Siempre traigo mi permiso de manejar.
   Hoy no ______________ el permiso conmigo.
8. Normalmente me pones tranquilo.
   Ahora ______________ nervioso.
9. Generalmente, Andrés duerme en casa.
   No sé por qué ahora ______________ en el coche.
10. En este restaurante siempre pedimos la paella.
    Pero esta noche ______________ la tortilla española.

Go Online WEB CODE jdd-0316
PHSchool.com

Repaso

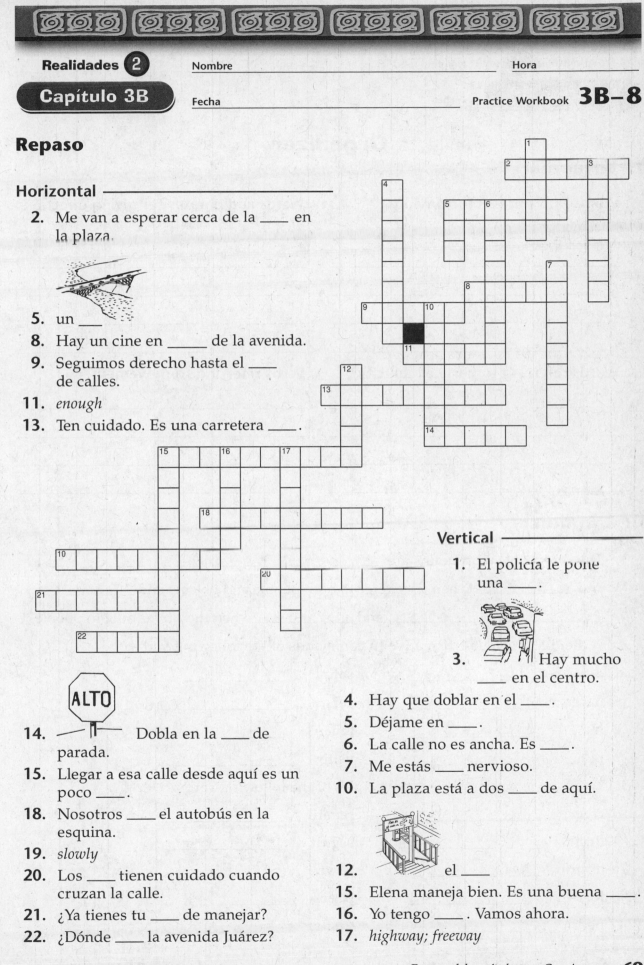

Horizontal

2. Me van a esperar cerca de la ___ en la plaza.
5. un ___
8. Hay un cine en _____ de la avenida.
9. Seguimos derecho hasta el ___ de calles.
11. *enough*
13. Ten cuidado. Es una carretera ____.
14. Dobla en la ____ de parada.
15. Llegar a esa calle desde aquí es un poco ____.
18. Nosotros ____ el autobús en la esquina.
19. *slowly*
20. Los ____ tienen cuidado cuando cruzan la calle.
21. ¿Ya tienes tu ____ de manejar?
22. ¿Dónde ____ la avenida Juárez?

ALTO

Vertical

1. El policía le pone una ____.
3. Hay mucho ____ en el centro.
4. Hay que doblar en el ____.
5. Déjame en ____.
6. La calle no es ancha. Es ____.
7. Me estás ____ nervioso.
10. La plaza está a dos ____ de aquí.
12. el ____
15. Elena maneja bien. Es una buena ____.
16. Yo tengo ____. Vamos ahora.
17. *highway; freeway*

Organizer

I. Vocabulary

Words and phrases for driving

______
______
______
______
______

Words and phrases for giving directions

______
______
______
______
______

Words referring to parts of the city

______
______
______
______

Verbs referring to movement

______
______
______
______

II. Grammar

1. The direct object pronouns are: ______, ______, ______, and ______ when they refer to both people and objects and ______, ______, ______, and ______ when they refer only to people.
2. Write the irregular affirmative **tú** commands of the following verbs:

decir	______	**salir**	______
hacer	______	**ser**	______
ir	______	**tener**	______
poner	______	**venir**	______

3. Write the irregular present participles of the following verbs:

creer	______	**repetir**	______
decir	______	**seguir**	______
dormir	______	**servir**	______
leer	______	**traer**	______
pedir	______	**vestir**	______

A ver si recuerdas...

¿Qué comida hay?

A. Read the following descriptions and decide which family member is being described. Write the correct word in the blank. Follow the model.

Modelo Es el hermano de mi padre. Es mi *tío*.

1. Son los padres de mis tíos. Son mis ______.
2. Es la hija de mi tía. Es mi ______.
3. Es el primo de mi hermana. Es mi ______.
4. Son los hijos de mis abuelos, pero no son mis padres. Son mis ______.
5. Es el único (*only*) hermano de mi tío. Es mi ______.
6. Son los hijos de mis padres. Son mis ______.
7. Es el padre de la hermana de mi madre. Es mi ______.

B. All of your family members are chipping in to help set up for dinner. Complete each sentence by telling what each family member is bringing to the table according to the pictures on the right.

1. Mi hermanito trae ______.
2. Mis primos traen ______.
3. Yo traigo ______.
4. Mi hermana mayor trae ______.
5. Mis abuelos traen ______.

WEB CODE jdd-0401

Realidades 2

Capítulo 4A

Nombre ______________________ Hora ____________

Fecha ______________________ Practice Workbook **4A–B**

A ver si recuerdas...

Es una fiesta

A. Look at the drawings of a birthday celebration and write what the subjects below are doing.

1. Emilia, Carlos y Víctor ______________________.
2. Mariana ______________________.
3. Martín ______________________.
4. Felisa y Bárbara ______________________.
5. La madre de Marta ______________________.
6. El tío Guillermo ______________________.

B. Change the underlined word or phrase in each of the following sentences without changing the meaning of the sentence. Then, write the new word on the blank. Follow the model.

Modelo Jorge es muy popular. *popularísimo*.

1. La tarea es muy fácil. ______________.
2. Jorge es mi hermano menor. ______________.
3. Los pantalones son muy grandes. ______________.
4. Esta comida es muy rica. ______________.
5. No quiero un sándwich tan pequeño. ______________.
6. Vamos a visitar a la abuela. ______________.

Nombre ______ Hora ______

Fecha ______ Practice Workbook **4A–1**

Acciones habituales

A. Complete the following sentences logically using words from the bank. Not all of the words will be used.

colección	generosa	molestar	bloques	vecino
oso	tren	tímida	triciclo	saltar

1. De niño me gustaba hacer casas y carreteras con mis ______.
2. A los tres años Claudia ya sabía montar en ______.
3. Pablo siempre duerme con su ______ de peluche.
4. Mi hermanita tiene una ______ de muñecas.
5. A mí me gusta ______ a la cuerda.
6. Isabel siempre comparte su comida con nosotros. Es muy ______.
7. Mi ______ me ayuda a cuidar a mi perro.
8. El juguete favorito de mi hermanito es su ______ eléctrico.

B. Complete the analogies below with words from your vocabulary.

1. salir : llegar :: prohibir : ______
2. lavar : limpiar :: compartir : ______
3. la voz : el coro :: un país : ______
4. cierto : falso :: nadie : ______
5. entusiasmado : emocionado :: reservado : ______

Nombre ______________ Hora ______________

Fecha ______________ Practice Workbook **4A–2**

¿Qué están haciendo?

Look at the drawings and tell what the people are doing.

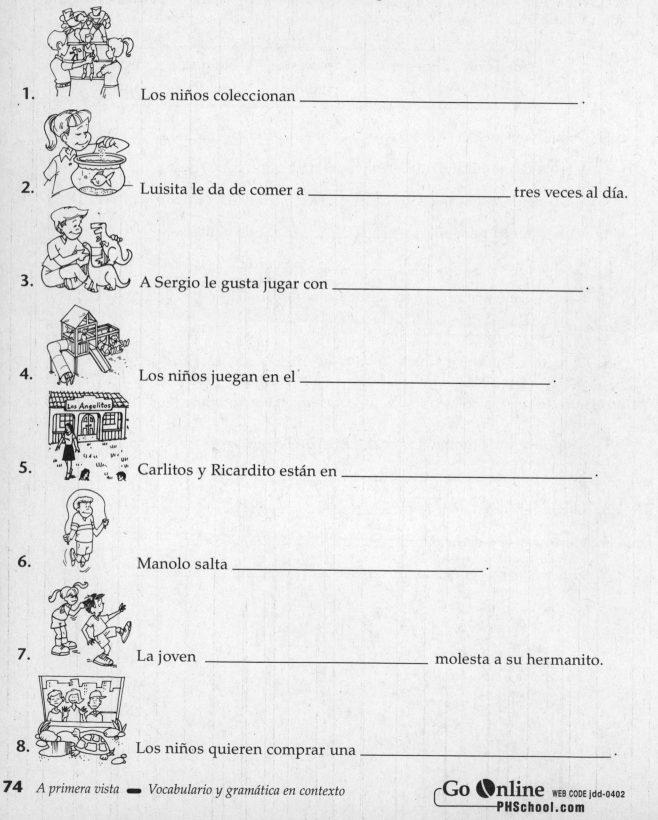

1. Los niños coleccionan ______________.

2. Luisita le da de comer a ______________ tres veces al día.

3. A Sergio le gusta jugar con ______________.

4. Los niños juegan en el ______________.

5. Carlitos y Ricardito están en ______________.

6. Manolo salta ______________.

7. La joven ______________ molesta a su hermanito.

8. Los niños quieren comprar una ______________.

Sinónimos y definiciones

A. Complete these sentences logically with adjectives from your vocabulary.

1. Ese niño siempre obedece. Es ________________.
2. A esa niña no le gusta hablar con la gente. Es ________________.
3. Los padres de Juan Pedro le compran todos los juguetes que pide. Por eso es ________________.
4. Rosa se porta muy bien con todos. Es una niña muy bien ________________.
5. Un niño que molesta a todo el mundo es muy ________________.

B. Complete these sentences logically with verbs from your vocabulary.

1. Parece que esos chicos no se llevan bien. Siempre se ________________.
2. Marcos es desobediente de vez en cuando, pero por lo general ________________ a sus padres.
3. Yo ________________ cuando no quiero decir la verdad.
4. No me gustan las personas que no se ________________ bien en un restaurante.
5. Mi hermano está durmiendo. No quiero ________________lo.
6. Mi amiga tiene casi cien muñecos. Le gusta ________________los.

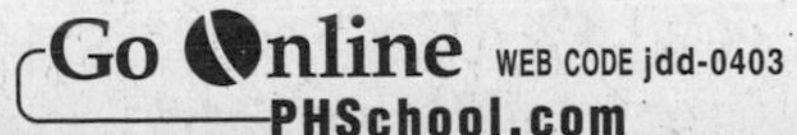

WEB CODE jdd-0403

Nombre ____________________ Hora ____________

Fecha ____________________ Practice Workbook **4A–4**

¿Qué hacen?

Based on the illustrations, write complete sentences to answer the questions about what the children are doing. Follow the model.

Modelo ¿En dónde se queda Jorgito durante el día?

Jorgito se queda en la guardería infantil durante el día.

1. ¿Qué tiene Margarita?

____.

2. ¿Con qué juega Marcos?

____.

3. ¿Con qué duerme siempre Pablo?

____.

4. ¿Qué les gusta hacer a las niñas?

____.

5. ¿Cómo se portan Raúl y Julia?

____.

6. ¿Qué sabe hacer Claudia a los tres años?

____.

7. ¿Qué le gusta hacer a Felipe?

____.

8. ¿Qué hacen siempre Diego y Pepe?

____.

Go Online WEB CODE jdd-0403
PHSchool.com

¿Qué hacían de pequeños?

The following people are talking about what they did in their youth. Write complete sentences to tell their stories. Follow the model.

Modelo Alicia *Alicia molestaba a sus hermanos menores*.

1. Mario ____
____.
2. Lorenzo y Alberto ____
____.
3. Tú ____
____.
4. Yo ____
____.
5. Tú y yo ____
____.
6. Tú ____
____.
7. Nosotras ____
____.
8. Luis y Sergio ____
____.
9. Yo ____
____.

Nombre _______________ Hora _______________

Fecha _______________ Practice Workbook **4A–6**

Así vivíamos

Martín and Susana are talking about what life was like when they were children and they lived in the country. To complete their thoughts, use the imperfect of the verbs **ir, ser,** and **ver.**

Mi familia y yo vivíamos en el campo. La casa _______________ muy grande. Mis abuelos vivían con nosotros. Ellos _______________ pelirrojos cuando nosotros _______________ jóvenes.

Cada día nosotros _______________ a pie a la escuela. Tú _______________ todo lo que pasaba en el camino a la escuela. Nuestro perro, Rey, _______________ con nosotros a la escuela. Él _______________ un perro muy obediente. En la escuela tú _______________ obediente, y entonces _______________ la estudiante favorita del profesor.

Después de la escuela yo _______________ a la casa de mis amigos Héctor y Elías. Por la mañana ellos _______________ de pesca con su padre, pero por la tarde nosotros _______________ al lago a nadar. Por la noche ellos _______________ la tele y yo me quedaba con mi familia. No teníamos mucho, pero _______________ felices.

Go Online WEB CODE jdd-0405
PHSchool.com

Nombre _______________ Hora _______________

Fecha _______________ Practice Workbook **4A–7**

¡Regalos!

Look at the pictures and use the verb **dar** and the appropriate indirect object pronoun to tell what gifts people are buying for each other. Follow the model.

Modelo  tú/a Juanito

Tú le das un tren eléctrico a Juanito _______________.

1.  nosotros/a Mónica

_______________.

2. 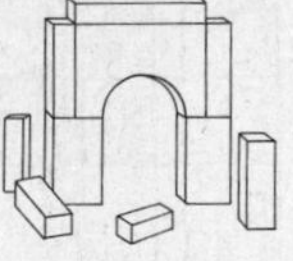 yo/a los niños

_______________.

3.  mis padres/a mí

_______________.

4.  mi hermana/a mi padre

_______________.

5.  tus padres/a ti

_______________.

6.  nuestros amigos/a nosotros

_______________.

7. 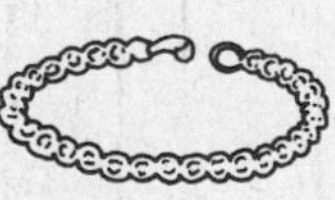 yo/a mi novia

_______________.

Go Online WEB CODE jdd-0406
PHSchool.com

Nombre ______________________ Hora ____________

Fecha ______________________ Practice Workbook **4A–8**

Repaso

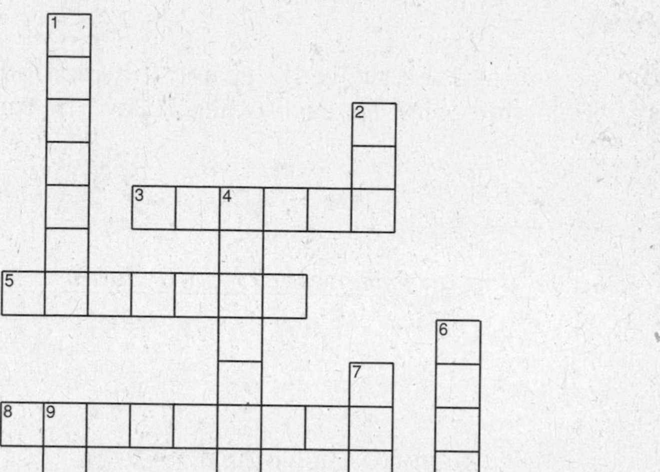

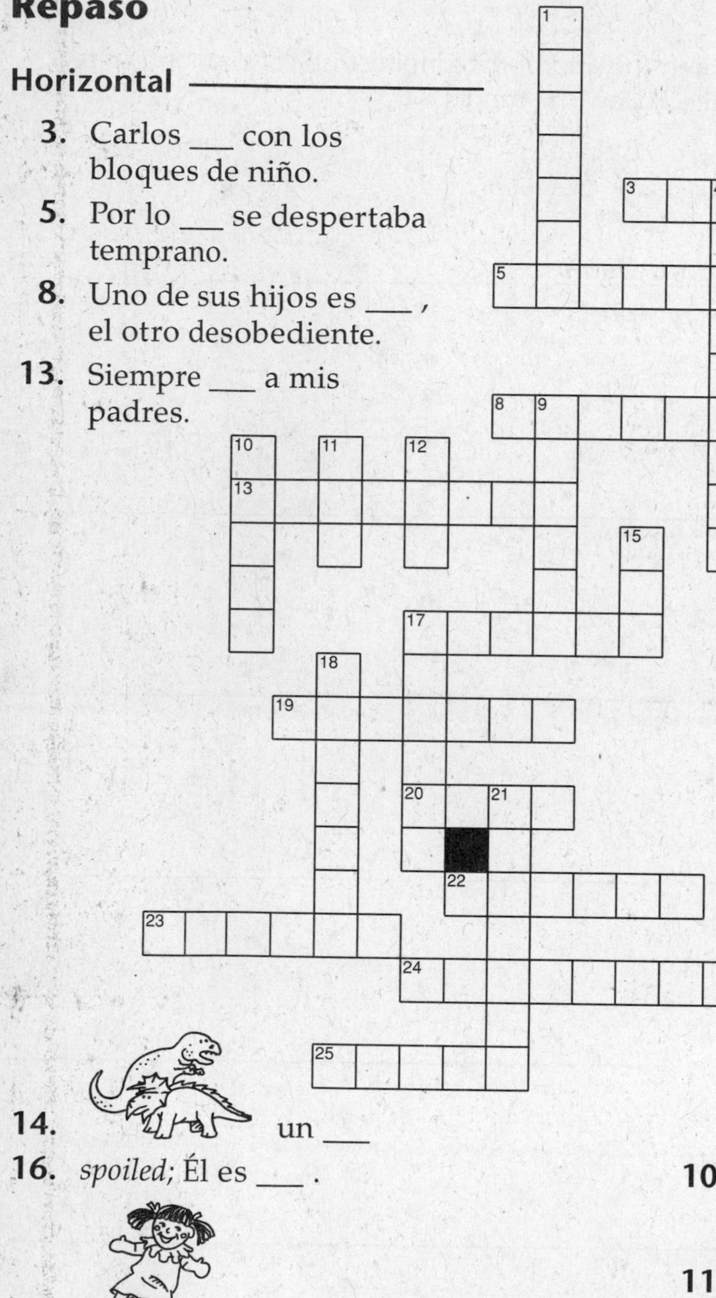

Horizontal

3. Carlos ___ con los bloques de niño.
5. Por lo ___ se despertaba temprano.
8. Uno de sus hijos es ___ , el otro desobediente.
13. Siempre ___ a mis padres.
14. un ___
16. *spoiled;* Él es ___ .
17. la ___
19. Todo le ___ . No está contento.
20. Jugábamos con el ___ eléctrico.
22. Saltaban a la ___ .
23. Estos chicos traviesos se ___ mucho.
24. Era un niño muy ___ . Se portaba mal.
25. Los chicos jugaban en el ___ de recreo.

Vertical

1. La niña no puede dormir sin su oso de ___ .
2. Jaime ___ travieso de niño.
4. Los niños están en la ___ infantil.
6. La niña se portaba bien con todo el ___ .
7. Nuestro ___ no está en casa.
9. *a block;* un ___
10. Lorenzo se ___ muy bien.
11.  Un ___ nada en el lago.
12. A ellos ___ gusta tu colección.
15. Paco ___ de pesca cuando era niño.
17. Ramona no dice la verdad. Ella ___ .
18. una ___
21. Es un niño bien ___ .

Nombre ____________________ Hora ________

Fecha ____________________ Practice Workbook **4A–9**

Organizer

I. Vocabulary

Words for toys

____
____
____
____
____

Words for personal qualities

____
____
____
____
____

Favorite pets

______________________ ______________________
______________________ ______________________

II. Grammar

1. Give the imperfect forms of these verbs.

jugar		permitir	
________	________	________	________
________	________	________	________
________	________	________	________

ser		ir	
________	________	________	________
________	________	________	________
________	________	________	________

2. To tell to whom or for whom an action is done, you use the ______________ pronouns. These are: ____________, ____________, ____________, ____________, ____________, ____________.

Realidades 2

Capítulo 4B

Nombre ____________________ Hora ____________

Fecha ____________________ Practice Workbook **4B–1**

¿Qué pasa?

Tell what these people are doing by filling in the missing words from the word bank. Not all of the words will be used.

lloran	**nació**	**se ríen**
fuegos artificiales	**modales**	**parientes**
reunión	**cuentan**	**antiguo**
cumplió		**había**
fiesta de sorpresa		**se reúnen**

1. Hay una ____________________ de la familia en casa de los abuelos el domingo.
2. Los chicos ____________________ cuando les cuento chistes.
3. El bebé ____________________ la semana pasada.
4. Elena y Tomás ____________________ a las nueve cada noche en la Plaza Mayor.
5. Berta no sabía que la ____________________ era para ella.
6. A la gente estadounidense le gusta ver los ____________________ para celebrar el cuatro de julio.
7. Para los días festivos todos los ____________________ se reúnen y hablan de cuando eran niños.
8. Muchas personas ____________________ en una boda porque están contentos.
9. Un regalo bueno para la boda es un reloj ____________________.
10. Mi padre ____________________ sesenta años el mes pasado.

¿Cuál es la costumbre?

A. Complete each of the following analogies with a word from your vocabulary.

1. niños : bebés :: ancianos : ____________
2. abrir : cerrar :: despedir : ____________
3. llevar : traer :: pasarlo bien : ____________
4. flojo : apretado :: pequeño : ____________
5. siempre : de vez en cuando :: nunca : ____________

B. Tell what the following people do every day.

1. Tito y Celia se ____________.

2. Paco se ____________ de Ramón.

3. Nieves y Lorena se ____________.

4. Gabriel le ____________ al amigo de Josefina.

5. Marta y Paco se ____________ en la fiesta.

6. Alejandro ____________ cuando se reúne con los parientes.

Nombre ______ Hora ______

Fecha ______ Practice Workbook **4B–3**

Falta una palabra

Complete the following sentences with the missing word.

1. La Navidad y el cuatro de julio son días ___ ___ ___ ___ ___ _v_ ___ ___.
2. Juan siempre ___ _u_ ___ ___ ___ ___ muchos chistes.
3. Cuando mis padres llegaron a la fiesta para su aniversario, todos gritamos,

   ¡___ ___ ___ ___ ___ ___ _d_ ___ _d_ ___ ___!
4. Álvaro mostró buenos _m_ ___ ___ ___ ___ ___ ___ porque charló con toda la gente.
5. La ___ ___ ___ _é_ nació ayer en el hospital .
6. Los hermanos se ___ ___ ___ _v_ ___ ___ muy bien. Nunca pelean.
7. El domingo vamos a hacer ___ _n_ ___ ___ ___ _n_ ___ ___. Tenemos mucha comida y va a hacer buen tiempo.
8. Marta caminó ___ ___ _r_ ___ ___ ___ ___ ___ _r_ del parque tres veces.
9. No _r_ ___ ___ ___ ___ ___ ___ ___ _o_ qué hicimos para el seis de enero. Quizás tuvimos una fiesta.
10. Mis parientes siempre ___ ___ ___ _r_ _l_ ___ ___ con sus amigos por teléfono.

Realidades 2 | Nombre ______ | Hora ______

Capítulo 4B | Fecha ______ | Practice Workbook **4B–4**

Días festivos entre familia

Isabel's favorite holiday is July 4th. Read her description of what they do every year in her town and then answer the questions that follow.

Hoy es mi día favorito. . . es el Día de la Independencia. Cada año mi familia y yo nos reunimos con los vecinos y vamos al centro para ver el desfile. A mucha gente de mi pueblo le gustan los desfiles. Hay algunos que los esperan en un parque cerca del centro. Ellos hacen unos picnics allí donde comen de todo.

En la Gran Vía (*Main Street*) todo el mundo está charlando en anticipación de las carrozas (*floats*) y las bandas musicales. También hay mucha gente importante del pueblo que camina entre las carrozas y bandas. Estas personas sonríen, saludan a la gente y a veces besan a los bebés. Los espectadores se ríen y se divierten mucho mientras que pasa el enorme desfile.

Después del desfile se reúne casi todo el pueblo en el parque. Allí conocemos a gente nueva y hablamos con los viejos amigos. Una vez conocí a las personas que encienden los fuegos artificiales. ¡Me permitieron encender unos pequeños!

1. En tu opinión, ¿a Isabel le gustan los días festivos? ¿Cuál es su día favorito?

____

____.

2. Describe qué hace la gente antes del desfile.

____

____.

3. ¿Qué pasa durante el desfile?

____

____.

4. ¿Toda la gente regresa a sus casas al final del desfile? Si no, ¿qué hacen?

____

____.

5. ¿Qué le pasó a Isabel una vez?

____

____.

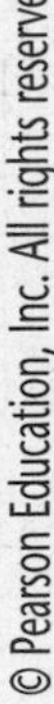

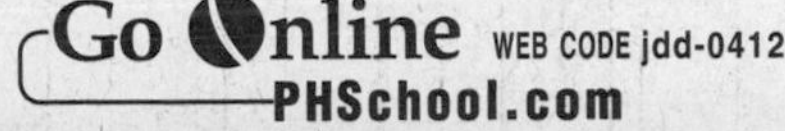

Reunión de familia

Amalia describes how wonderful the family gatherings were when she was a child. Complete her story with the imperfect of the appropriate verbs in parentheses. The first one is done for you.

Cuando yo ___*era*___ (hablar / ser) niña, mis parientes ______ (conocer / reunirse) los domingos en casa de mi abuela. Mi abuela ______ (preparar / llamar) mucha comida y mi madre y mis tías la ______ (pensar / ayudar). Yo ______ (pedir / jugar) con mis primos. Todos nosotros ______ (llevarse / llegar) muy bien, y ______ (divertirse / escuchar) mucho. Nosotros ______ (ver / almorzar) juntos (*together*), ______ (contar / ir) chistes y ______ (reírse / conocer) tanto. Mi primo Raúl siempre ______ (jugar / traer) la guitarra. Él ______ (tocar / traer) muy bien y nos ______ (gustar / casarse) escucharlo. Nosotros ______ (llamar / cantar) nuestras canciones favoritas. Todos en la familia ______ (ver / quedarse) en casa de la abuela hasta las nueve de la noche y después ______ (regresar / sacar) a casa, cansados, pero muy contentos. Todavía pienso mucho en esas maravillosas reuniones de familia.

Go Online WEB CODE jdd-0413 PHSchool.com

Nombre ______________________ Hora ____________

Fecha ______________________ Practice Workbook **4B–6**

Entre amigos

Write a complete sentence telling what the friends in each illustration are doing. Use reflexive pronouns. Follow the model.

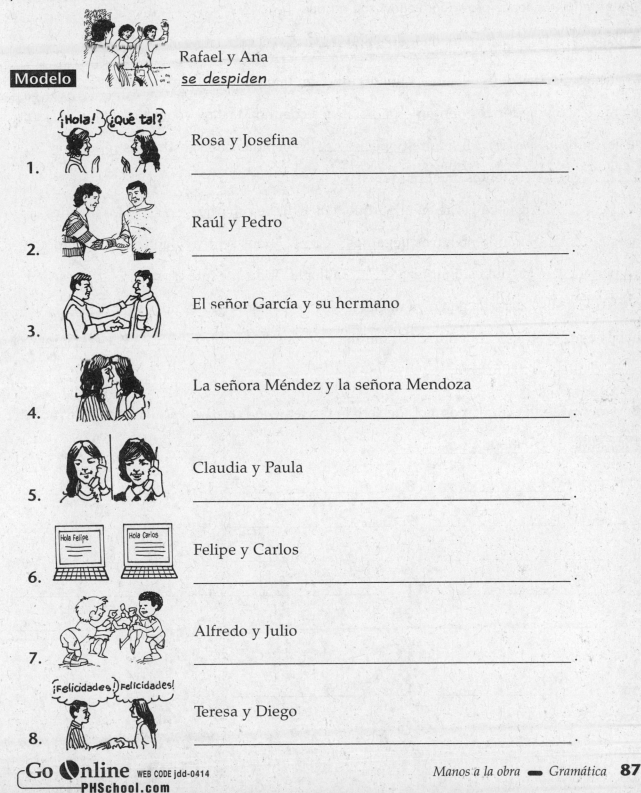

Modelo 

Rafael y Ana
se despiden __________.

1. ¡Hola! ¿Qué tal?
Rosa y Josefina
______________________.

2. Raúl y Pedro
______________________.

3. 
El señor García y su hermano
______________________.

4. 
La señora Méndez y la señora Mendoza
______________________.

5. 
Claudia y Paula
______________________.

6. 

Felipe y Carlos
______________________.

7. 
Alfredo y Julio
______________________.

8. 

Teresa y Diego
______________________.

Nombre ____________________ Hora ________

Fecha ____________________ Practice Workbook **4B–7**

Lo que hicimos ayer

A. Read the description below about something that happened in the past. Decide whether the underlined verbs should be in the preterite or imperfect. Write *I* for imperfect and *P* for preterite in the space provided. Follow the model.

Modelo Hace __I__ sol cuando salgo __P__.

Un día, cuando hace ______ buen tiempo, mi familia y yo decidimos ______ hacer un picnic. Paco y Federico cuentan ______ chistes cuando Marta y yo encontramos ______ la cesta (*picnic basket*). Mi madre pone ______ las bebidas en la cesta. Nos reunimos ______ con los parientes en el parque.

Hay ______ mucha gente en el parque. Los mayores charlan ______ y los jóvenes juegan ______ cuando nosotros llegamos ______. Todos se divierten ______ cuando vienen ______ las nubes. Empieza ______ a llover. Toda la gente corre ______ a sus coches o a sus casas. La gente ya no se ríe ______, los jóvenes ya no juegan ______ y los bebés empiezan ______ a llorar. Mi familia y yo nos despedimos ______ y así termina ______ nuestro día festivo.

B. Now, write the correct form of the verb in the tense indicated in Part A. Follow the model.

Modelo *Hacía / salí*

1. ____________ 8. ____________ 15. ____________
2. ____________ 9. ____________ 16. ____________
3. ____________ 10. ____________ 17. ____________
4. ____________ 11. ____________ 18. ____________
5. ____________ 12. ____________ 19. ____________
6. ____________ 13. ____________
7. ____________ 14. ____________

Go Online WEB CODE jdd-0416
PHSchool.com

Repaso

Horizontal

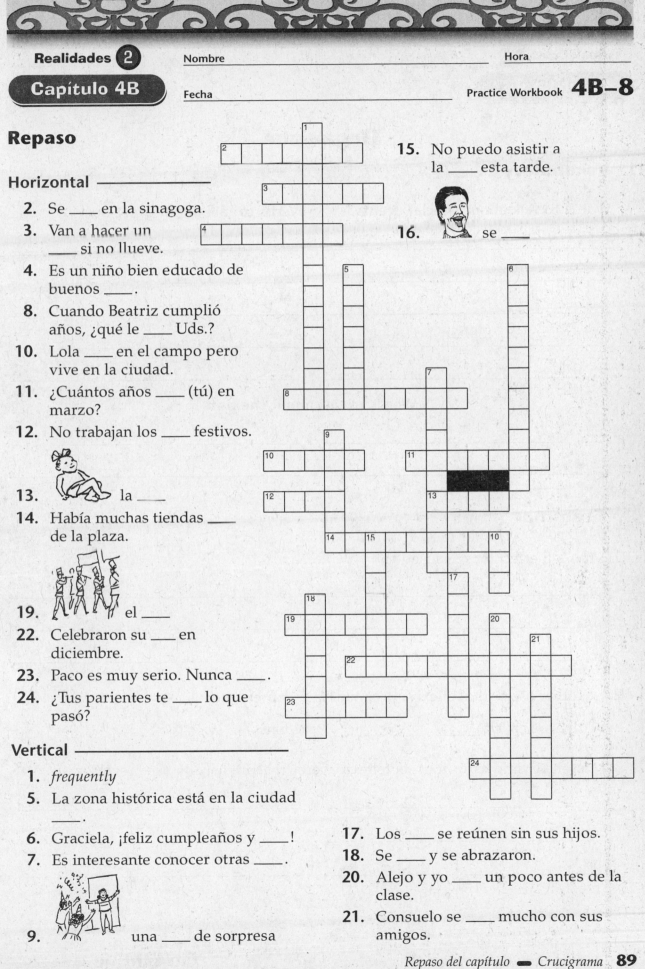

2. Se ____ en la sinagoga.
3. Van a hacer un ____ si no llueve.
4. Es un niño bien educado de buenos ____.
8. Cuando Beatriz cumplió años, ¿qué le ____ Uds.?
10. Lola ____ en el campo pero vive en la ciudad.
11. ¿Cuántos años ____ (tú) en marzo?
12. No trabajan los ____ festivos.
13. la ____
14. Había muchas tiendas ____ de la plaza.
15. No puedo asistir a la ____ esta tarde.
16. se ____
19. el ____
22. Celebraron su ____ en diciembre.
23. Paco es muy serio. Nunca ____.
24. ¿Tus parientes te ____ lo que pasó?

Vertical

1. *frequently*
5. La zona histórica está en la ciudad ____.
6. Graciela, ¡feliz cumpleaños y ____!
7. Es interesante conocer otras ____.
9.  una ____ de sorpresa
17. Los ____ se reúnen sin sus hijos.
18. Se ____ y se abrazaron.
20. Alejo y yo ____ un poco antes de la clase.
21. Consuelo se ____ mucho con sus amigos.

Nombre ______ Hora ______

Fecha ______ Practice Workbook **4B–9**

Organizer

I. Vocabulary

Words to talk about special events | **Verbs to talk about greetings**

______ ______
______ ______
______ ______
______ ______
______ ______

Words to talk about the past

______ ______
______ ______

II. Grammar

1. The imperfect tense is used to

a. ______

b. ______

c. ______

2. Another use of the reflexive pronouns is to express the idea "(to) each other." These are called ______ actions.

3. List the infinitive form of six reflexive verbs that are usually used reciprocally.

______ ______
______ ______
______ ______

A ver si recuerdas...

¿Qué ves en los cuartos?

Look at the drawings to find out what items can be seen in the house.

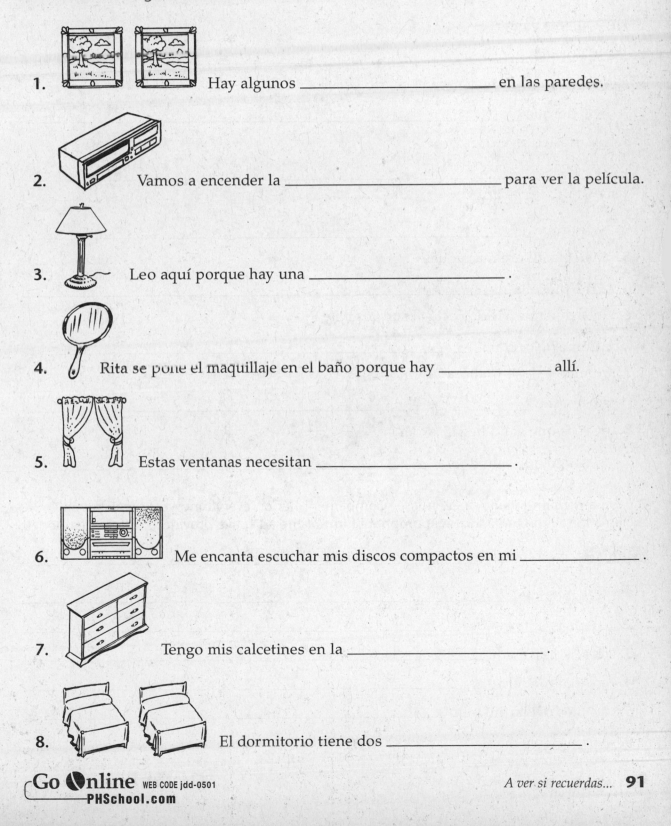

1. Hay algunos ______________ en las paredes.

2. Vamos a encender la ______________ para ver la película.

3. Leo aquí porque hay una ______________.

4. Rita se pone el maquillaje en el baño porque hay ______________ allí.

5. Estas ventanas necesitan ______________.

6. Me encanta escuchar mis discos compactos en mi ______________.

7. Tengo mis calcetines en la ______________.

8. El dormitorio tiene dos ______________.

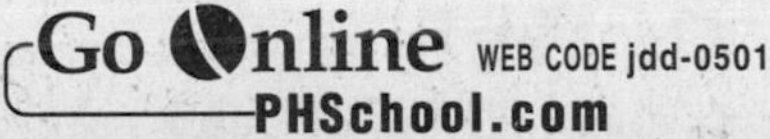

WEB CODE jdd-0501

Realidades 2

Capítulo 5A

Nombre ______________________ Hora ______________________

Fecha ______________________ Practice Workbook **5A–B**

A ver si recuerdas...

¿Tienes ganas?

A. Respond to each question using an expression with **tener.**

1. ¿Quieres comer?

   Sí, porque ______________________.
2. ¿El niño quiere entrar en el cuarto oscuro?

   No, porque ______________________.
3. ¿Carlos es joven?

   Sí, ______________ 15 ______________.
4. ¿Quieres tu abrigo?

   Sí, porque ______________________.
5. Marcela quiere más agua.

   Creo que ella ______________________.
6. José dijo que México está al sur de Chile.

   ¿Cómo? No, él no ______________________.
7. ¿Quieres dormir ahora?

   Sí, porque ______________________.
8. ¿Crees que vas a llegar tarde?

   Sí, tengo que salir ahora. ______________________.

B. You are visiting Paula's new house. Compliment her on everything you see using an exclamation with **Qué** and the appropriate form of the adjective provided. Follow the model.

Modelo casa/nuevo *¡Qué nueva es la casa!*

1. sala/bonito ______________________
2. cuadros/interesante ______________________
3. televisor/grande ______________________
4. cocina/moderno ______________________
5. árboles del jardín/alto ______________________
6. cortinas/elegante ______________________

Go Online
WEB CODE jdd-0501
PHSchool.com

Realidades 2 | Nombre ______ | Hora ______

Capítulo 5A | Fecha ______ | Practice Workbook **5A–1**

Un desastre

Tell what happened when a fire broke out by using the drawings to complete the sentences with the missing words.

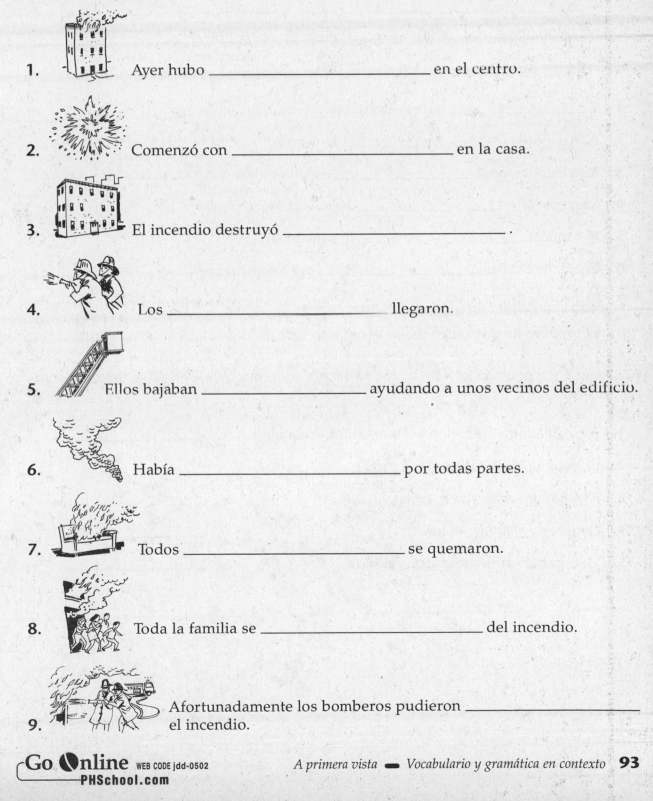

1. Ayer hubo ____________________ en el centro.
2. Comenzó con ____________________ en la casa.
3. El incendio destruyó ____________________ .
4. Los ____________________ llegaron.
5. Ellos bajaban ____________________ ayudando a unos vecinos del edificio.
6. Había ____________________ por todas partes.
7. Todos ____________________ se quemaron.
8. Toda la familia se ____________________ del incendio.
9.  Afortunadamente los bomberos pudieron ____________________ el incendio.

Realidades 2 | Nombre ______ | Hora ______

Capítulo 5A | Fecha ______ | Practice Workbook **5A–2**

¿Qué ocurrió?

A. Find out what disasters befell one area by filling in the missing verbs from the newscast below. Not all of the words will be used.

destruyó	**apagaron**	**murieron**	**quemaron**	**rescatar**
esconderse	**sube**	**nevó**	**ocurrieron**	**llamaron**

1. ____________________ tres desastres ayer en esta región.
2. Nadie podía ____________________ del terror.
3. Muchas personas ____________________ a la policía pero no pudieron hacer nada.
4. Muchos se ____________________ a causa del terremoto.
5. El huracán ____________________ dos pueblos.
6. En las montañas ____________________ por veinticuatro horas.
7. Muchos edificios se ____________________ a causa de los incendios horribles.
8. El número de personas que se escaparon ____________________ cada hora.

B. Change the underlined word in each sentence to its opposite, and write the new word on the line.

1. Afortunadamente todos los habitantes están *vivos*. ____________________
2. El bombero *subió* la escalera. ____________________
3. El noticiero acaba de *terminar*. ____________________
4. Tengo que *encender* la luz. ____________________
5. La bombera trata de *destruir* la vida. ____________________

Go Online WEB CODE jdd-0502 PHSchool.com

Realidades 2 | Nombre ______________ | Hora ______________

Capítulo 5A | Fecha ______________ | Practice Workbook **5A–3**

Un desastre en Nicaragua

Complete the following conversation with logical words. Each dash represents a letter.

LAURA: ¿___ _y_ ___ _r_ ___ ___ ustedes lo que pasó en Nicaragua?

PABLO: No, no oímos nada. ¿Qué pasó?

LAURA: Llegó un ___ _u_ ___ ___ ___ ___ _n_ a la costa con vientos fuertes y mucha ___ ___ _u_ _v_ ___ ___.

CARLOS: Los huracanes son _t_ ___ ___ ___ ___ ___ _t_ ___ ___ terribles.

LAURA: También hubo muchas ___ _n_ ___ _n_ ___ ___ ___ ___ ___ _n_ ___ ___ porque ___ ___ _o_ ___ ___ _ó_ doce horas sin parar.

PABLO: ¿Se murió mucha gente?

LAURA: Todavía no se sabe. Están _i_ ___ ___ ___ ___ ___ _i_ ___ ___ ___ ___ _o_ ahora.

CARLOS: Me imagino que el huracán destruyó muchas casas.

LAURA: Sí, vi en el ___ _o_ ___ ___ ___ ___ ___ ___ _o_ que se destruyó un pueblo entero. Afortunadamente dicen que todo el mundo pudo ___ _s_ _c_ ___ ___ ___ ___ _s_ ___.

PABLO: ___ _i_ ___   ___ ___ ___ _a_ van a hablar del desastre en el noticiero de esta noche. Es muy importante.

LAURA: Creo que sí. Ya hay muchos _r_ ___ ___ ___ _r_ ___ ___ _r_ ___ ___ de todos los canales allí. Hablan con la gente que vive allí.

CARLOS: Vamos a comprar el periódico. Seguro que ya hay muchos ___ ___ ___ _í_ _c_ ___ ___ ___ _s_ sobre el huracán.

Nombre ______ Hora ______

Fecha ______ Practice Workbook **5A–4**

Una noticia terrible

Read the following news story and answer the questions below.

Ayer hubo un terremoto muy fuerte cerca de la ciudad. Creemos que muchas personas murieron y el terremoto también destruyó muchos edificios.

Después de investigar, la policía dice que ocurrió a las dos de la mañana. Toda la ciudad dormía cuando de repente comenzó un temblor (*shake*) enorme. Muchas personas asustadas gritaron mientras que otras trataron de llamar a la policía. La gente viva trató de ayudar a otras personas a escapar del peligro. Muchas personas valientes son los héroes del momento por rescatar a sus compañeros heridos de uno de los peores desastres en la historia de la ciudad.

1. ¿Qué cosa terrible ocurrió ayer?

   ______.

2. ¿Qué pudo decir la policía sobre el terremoto?

   ______.

3. ¿Había mucha gente por las calles cuando comenzó? Explica.

   ______

   ______.

4. ¿Qué hicieron las personas que sintieron el terremoto?

   ______.

5. ¿Cómo se compara este desastre con otros en la historia de la ciudad?

   ______

   ______.

6. ¿Por qué son héroes algunas personas?

   ______

   ______.

Go Online WEB CODE jdd-0503
PHSchool.com

Realidades 2 | Nombre ______ | Hora ______

Capítulo 5A | Fecha ______ | Practice Workbook **5A–5**

Un mal día

A. You are reading about Juanito's bad day yesterday. Decide whether the underlined verbs should be in the preterite or imperfect. Write **I** for imperfect and **P** for preterite. Follow the model.

Modelo Juanito tiene __I__ sed.

Juanito se despierta _____ temprano. Son _____ las seis de la mañana cuando se levanta _____ . No se siente _____ bien. Parece _____ que está _____ muy cansado. No duerme _____ bien anoche y en ese momento no quiere _____ comer. Dice _____ que está _____ enfermo. Todavía tiene _____ que ir a la escuela.

En la escuela es _____ un día muy feo. No puede _____ hacer la tarea. No quiere _____ ir afuera porque está _____ lloviendo. Sale _____ temprano de la escuela y se acuesta _____ cuando llega _____ a casa. Así terminó el día.

B. Now, write the correct form of each verb in the tense you have indicated above. Follow the model.

Modelo ______tenía______

1. ______ 7. ______ 13. ______
2. ______ 8. ______ 14. ______
3. ______ 9. ______ 15. ______
4. ______ 10. ______ 16. ______
5. ______ 11. ______ 17. ______
6. ______ 12. ______ 18. ______

Realidades 2 | **Capítulo 5A**

Nombre ______________________ Hora ______________

Fecha ______________________ Practice Workbook **5A–6**

¿Dónde fue eso?

Use the drawings to write sentences that tell where these things happened. Follow the model.

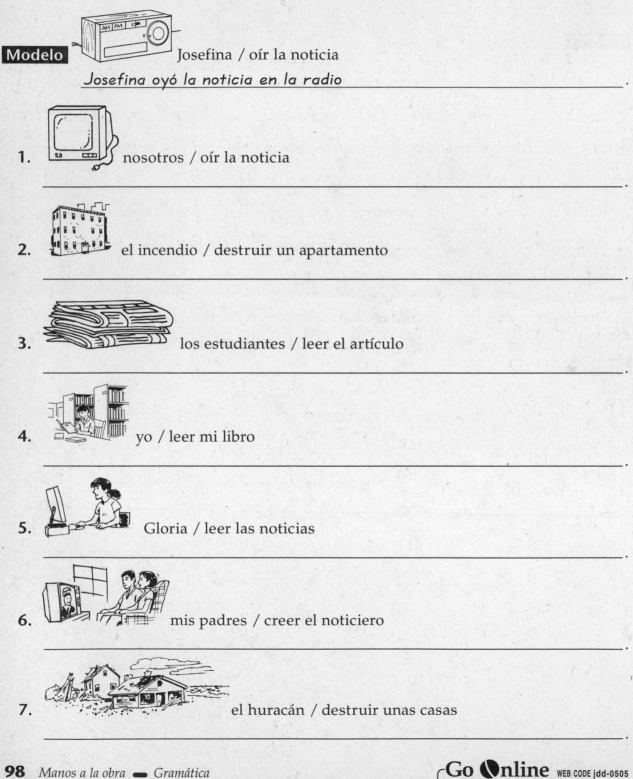

Modelo 

Josefina / oír la noticia

Josefina oyó la noticia en la radio.

1. 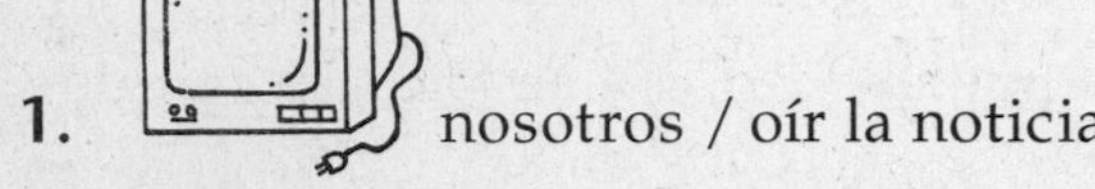 nosotros / oír la noticia

   ____.

2. 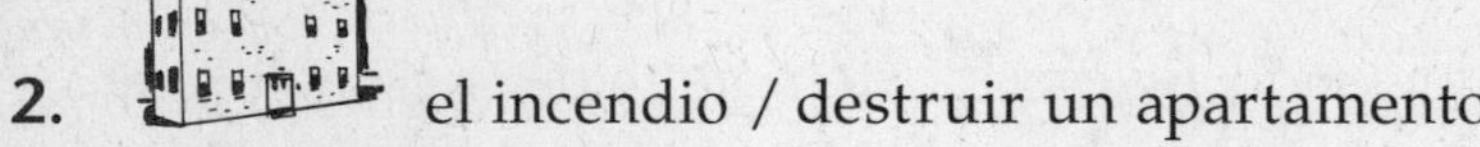 el incendio / destruir un apartamento

   ____.

3. 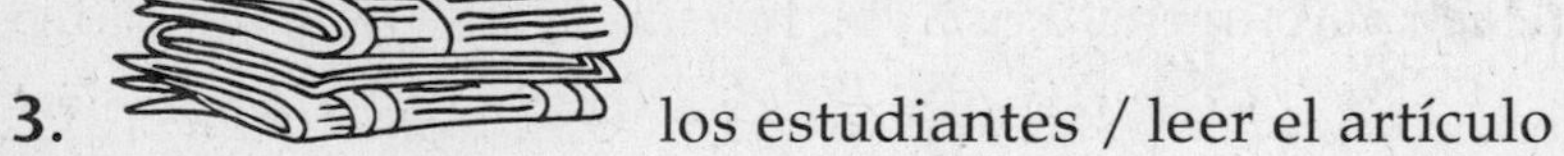 los estudiantes / leer el artículo

   ____.

4.  yo / leer mi libro

   ____.

5. 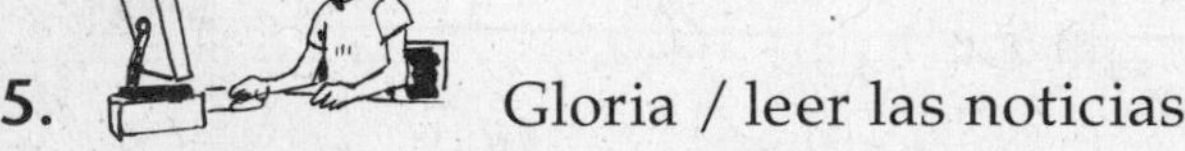 Gloria / leer las noticias

   ____.

6. 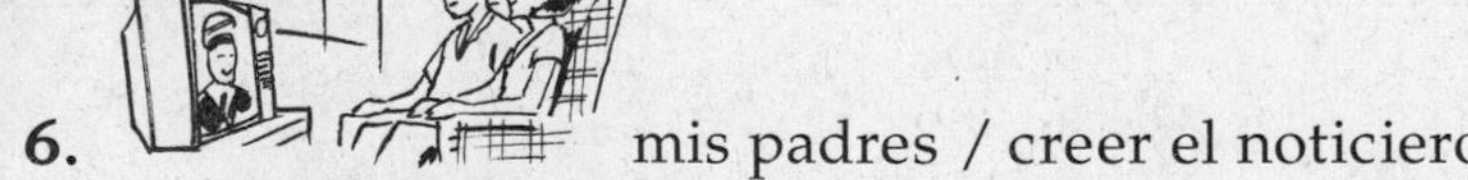 mis padres / creer el noticiero

   ____.

7.  el huracán / destruir unas casas

   ____.

Go Online WEB CODE jdd-0505
PHSchool.com

¿Qué pasó?

Your local television station's news reporters are investigating several stories from last night. Help them collect information by choosing a person from **Columna A,** a verb from **Columna B,** and a person or thing from **Columna C.** Put the verbs in the preterite tense to form complete sentences telling what happened last night. Follow the model.

Columna A	Columna B	Columna C
Yo	oír	los coches de la policía
Tú	creer que	una ventana
La Sra. Alfonso	leer	alguien entró en la casa
Enrique y Roberto	destruir	los perros ladrando (*barking*)
Nosotros		del ladrón en el periódico
El ladrón (*robber*)		el teléfono pero nadie contestó
Marisol y yo		todo el edificio
El incendio		una novela de horror

Modelo *La señora Alfonso oyó los perros ladrando.*

1. ______
2. ______
3. ______
4. ______
5. ______
6. ______
7. ______
8. ______

Repaso

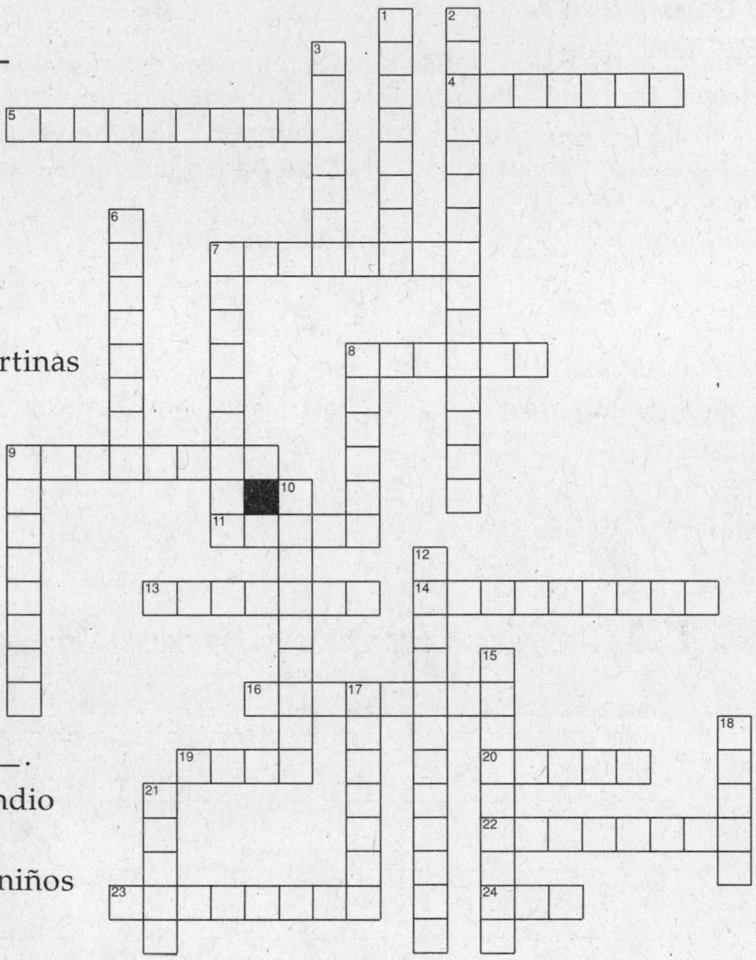

Horizontal

4. ¿Cuándo ___ el desastre?
5. El detective va a ___ el crimen.
7. Primero bajan y luego suben la ___.
8. Te voy a ___ por teléfono.
9. El niño se ___ detrás de las cortinas ayer.
11. ___ mucho en las montañas.
13. *Help!* ¡___! 
14. El ___ empieza a las seis.
16. Es muy tarde. Todos están ___.
19. Ricki sabía que hubo un incendio porque vio el ___.
20. Lorena les ___ la vida a unos niños en peligro.
22. *article;* el ___
23. Los ___ apagaron el incendio.
24. ¿Ud. ___ la explosión?

Vertical

1. El héroe es muy ___.
2. *fortunately*
3. Sandra rescató a muchos heridos. Es una ___.

6. un ___
7. El incendio comenzó con una ___.
8. Cayó mucha ___ anoche. Ahora todo está mojado.
9. Vivo en un ___ de apartamentos

10. Era un ___ fuerte.
12. Llovió mucho. Hubo ___.
15. Los empleados en la oficina estaban ___ por el terremoto.
17. Hay que comprar ___ para la casa nueva.
18. Hay más ___ que muertos.
21. Un ___ bueno tiene que ser valiente.

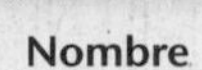

Realidades 2 Nombre Hora

Capítulo 5A Fecha Practice Workbook **5A–9**

Organizer

I. Vocabulary

Words to discuss rescues

Words for disasters and bad weather

Words to discuss the news

Words for talking about fires

II. Grammar

1. What tense is used to describe physical, mental, and emotional states in the past?

2. Give the preterite forms of these verbs.

oír **creer**

leer **destruir**

Nombre ______ Hora ______

Fecha ______

En el consultorio

A. Find out what happened at the doctor's office by selecting the correct word or words from each pair of words in parentheses. Write the correct word in the blank.

1. El médico ____________ al niño. (examinó/dio)
2. Al señor Tamayo le ____________ los músculos. (tropezaban/dolían)
3. Esteban se rompió un ____________ de la mano. (tobillo/hueso)
4. La médica ____________ unas medicinas. (recetó/dolió)
5. El enfermero le pone una ____________ a la señora García. (rodilla/inyección)
6. El niño tiene que llevar un ____________. (yeso/cuello)
7. La enfermera sacó ____________. (muñecas/radiografías)
8. El médico le ____________ a Rebeca. (dio puntadas/qué lástima)

B. Read the following descriptions, and write the vocabulary word that best fits each one.

1. Conecta la mano con el brazo. ____________
2. Parte del brazo entre el hombro y la mano. ____________
3. Parte de la pierna entre la rodilla y el pie. ____________
4. Cuando hay un accidente, esto lleva a los heridos a la sala de emergencia.

   ____
5. Si te cortas, puede salir esto. ____________
6. Unas pastillas para el dolor son un ejemplo de esto. ____________

Go Online WEB CODE jdd-0511
PHSchool.com

Los accidentes

Tell what is happening during a busy day in the emergency room by writing the missing word or words in the space provided. Use a different picture to help you each time.

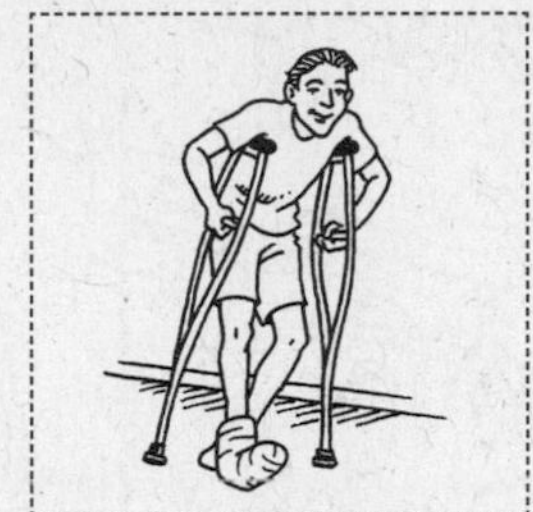

1. Juan se cayó jugando al fútbol. Le duele ______________________.
2. Perla chocó con otra patinadora y se lastimó ______________________.
3. Martín necesita usar ______________________ para caminar.
4. La enfermera le pone una ______________________ a Paquito.
5. Jorge y Claudia son ______________________ en el hospital.
6. Ramón tiene que usar una ______________________.
7. La médica le da una ______________________ a Isabel porque se lastimó la pierna.
8. Elisa va a visitar a una amiga en la ______________________.

Nombre ____________________ Hora ____________

Fecha ____________________ Practice Workbook **5B–3**

El accidente de Diego

Complete the following conversation between Ana and Lucía about Diego's accident. Use the pictures to help you.

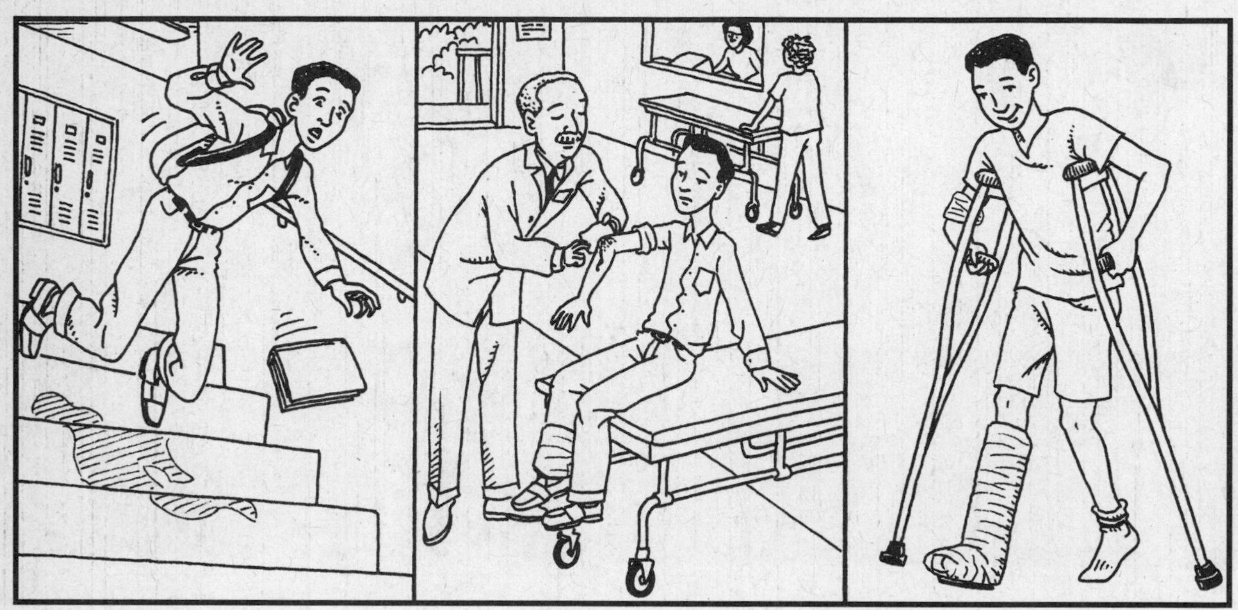

ANA: ¿No sabes qué le ____________________ a Diego?

LUCÍA: No, no sé nada. Dime.

ANA: ____________________ con la escalera en el colegio y ____________________.

LUCÍA: ¡Qué horror! ¿Se ____________________ mucho?

ANA: Oh, sí. Le ____________________ todo el cuerpo, sobre todo la pierna. Tuvieron que llevarlo al hospital.

LUCÍA: No lo puedo creer. ¿Está bien?

ANA: No del todo. Se ____________________ el codo y le pusieron una venda. Y le dijeron que tenía la pierna ____________________ y que va a tener que caminar con ____________________.

LUCÍA: ¿Tiene que llevar ____________________?

ANA: Sí, por un mes.

LUCÍA: ¡Qué ____________________!

Un desastre

Read the following story about a day when many people were injured. Then, answer the questions that follow in complete sentences.

Parecía un día normal, pero después del primer accidente, todo resultó un desastre. Los Suárez trabajaban en la casa. El papá estaba subiendo la escalera cuando Paquito chocó con ella. El papá se cayó al suelo y Paquito también se cayó. Los dos se lastimaron. El papá se torció el tobillo y la espalda. Paquito tenía una herida en la cabeza.

Luego, la mamá caminaba por el pasillo y sin ver a su hijo y a su esposo, tropezó con ellos. Ella llevaba un paquete que cayó y le hizo otra herida a Paquito. La mamá se cayó sobre el papá y los dos se lastimaron.

Cuando todos pudieron moverse otra vez, Sarita entró en el cuarto y les anunció que acababa de romperse la muñeca y tenía que ir a la sala de emergencia.

1. ¿Qué hacía la familia Suárez en este día tan horrible?

   ______.

2. ¿Cuál fue el primer "accidente"?

   ______

   ______.

3. ¿Qué le pasó a Paquito?

   ______.

4. ¿Cómo se sentía el papá después de caerse?

   ______.

5. ¿Qué le pasó a la mamá?

   ______.

6. ¿Dónde estaban los tres cuando entró Sarita?

   ______.

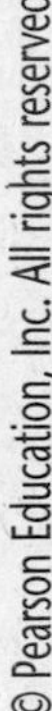

Realidades 2

Capítulo 5B

Nombre ____________________ Hora ____________

Fecha ____________________ Practice Workbook **5B–5**

El accidente de Luisa

Retell the story of Luisa's accident in the preterite. The first sentence has been done for you.

1.	Tengo un accidente.	Tuve un accidente.
2.	Me caigo en la escalera.	Me ____________ en la escalera.
3.	No puedo levantarme.	No ____________ levantarme.
4.	Viene la ambulancia.	____________ la ambulancia.
5.	Me lleva al hospital.	Me ____________ al hospital.
6.	Me traen una silla de ruedas.	Me ____________ una silla de ruedas.
7.	Los médicos me examinan.	Los médicos me ____________.
8.	Una enfermera me pone una venda en la cabeza.	Una enfermera me ____________ una venda en la cabeza.
9.	Los médicos me dicen que tenía la pierna rota.	Los médicos me ____________ que tenía la pierna rota.
10.	Ellos me ponen un yeso.	Ellos me ____________ un yeso.
11.	Me enseñan a caminar con muletas.	Me ____________ a caminar con muletas.
12.	Me recetan unas pastillas para el dolor.	Me ____________ unas pastillas para el dolor.
13.	Estoy tres horas en el hospital.	____________ tres horas en el hospital.

Nombre ______ Hora ______

Fecha ______ Practice Workbook **5B–6**

Todo el mundo estaba ocupado

Look at the drawings and complete the sentences telling what these people were doing at different times during the day yesterday. Use the imperfect progressive tense in your answers. Follow the model.

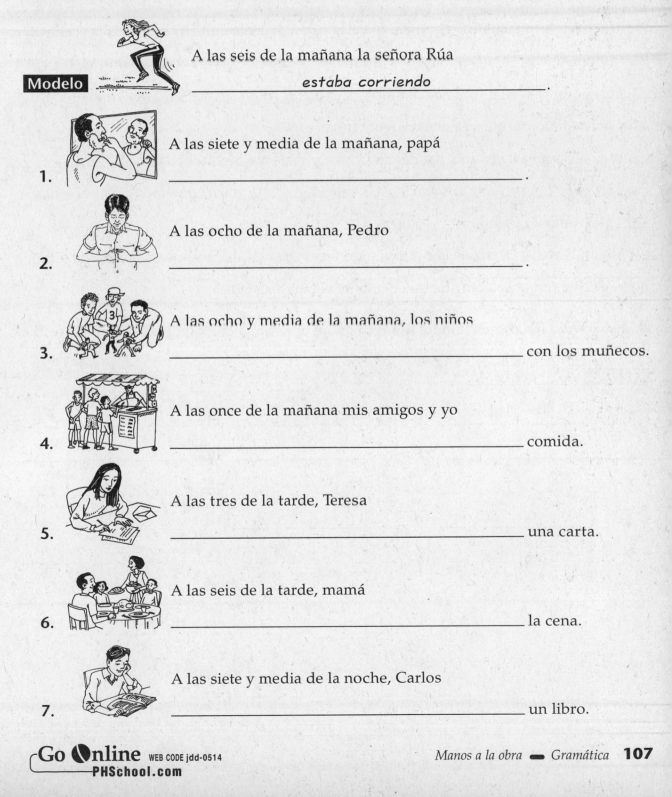

Modelo A las seis de la mañana la señora Rúa *estaba corriendo*.

1. A las siete y media de la mañana, papá ______.
2. A las ocho de la mañana, Pedro ______.
3. A las ocho y media de la mañana, los niños ______ con los muñecos.
4. A las once de la mañana mis amigos y yo ______ comida.
5. A las tres de la tarde, Teresa ______ una carta.
6. A las seis de la tarde, mamá ______ la cena.
7. A las siete y media de la noche, Carlos ______ un libro.

Nombre ______ Hora ______

Fecha ______ Practice Workbook **5B–7**

Lo que estaba pasando cuando...

A. Read the following paragraph. Then, read the paragraph again and decide whether each verb given should be in the preterite or imperfect progressive tense. Write either a **P** or an **I** in the blank that corresponds to the verb. The first one has been done for you.

Eran las cinco cuando __P__ (ocurrir) el accidente. Había mucha gente en las calles. Mis amigos y yo ____ (caminar) por una calle cuando ____ (ver) el accidente. Yo ____ (correr) entonces ____ (caerse) cuando ____ (oír) el ruido. Yo no ____ (lastimarse) pero estaba asustado porque era un accidente terrible.

Yo ____ (hablar) con mis padres más tarde y ellos me ____ (decir) que ____ (leer) cuando ____ (oír) chocar dos coches. Un reportero ____ (decir) que todas las personas ____ (lastimarse) y unos ____ (morir).

Mi abuela ____ (cruzar) la calle cuando un coche casi ____ (chocarse) con ella. Ella no tenía que ir a la sala de emergencia, pero estaba asustada.

B. Now, write the correct form of the verb in the tense you have indicated above. Follow the model.

Modelo ocurrió

1. ______
2. ______
3. ______
4. ______
5. ______
6. ______
7. ______
8. ______
9. ______
10. ______
11. ______
12. ______
13. ______
14. ______
15. ______

Go Online WEB CODE jdd-0516
PHSchool.com

Repaso

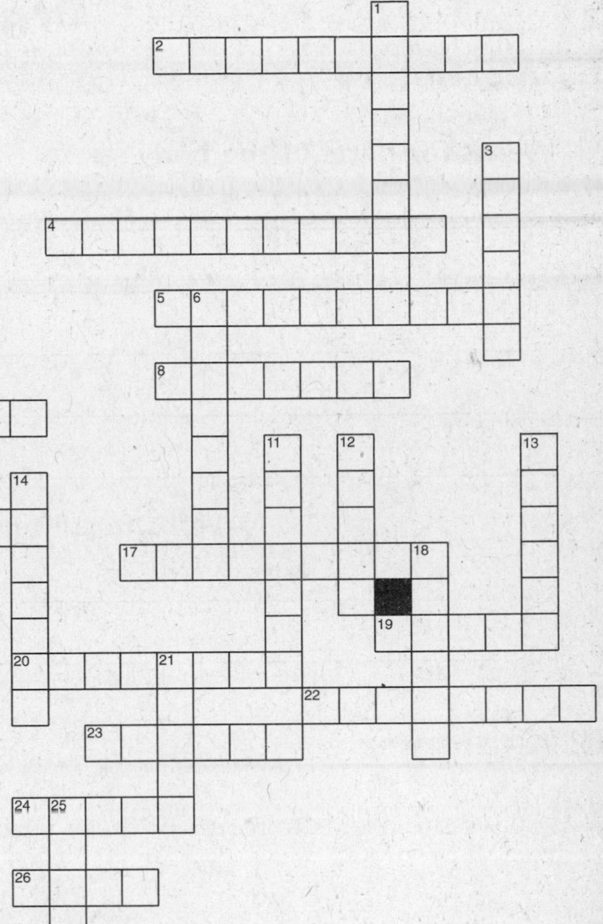

Horizontal

2. Está en la sala de ___.
4. El dentista saca una ___ de los dientes.
5. Llevan al enfermo al hospital en la ___.
8.  la ___
10. ¿La médica te ___ una pastillas ayer?
15. La ___ cuida a los enfermos.
17. Necesito tomar unas ___ para el dolor.
19. Te cortaste. Debes ponerte una ___.
20. *medicine*
22. María se cortó y le dieron ___.
23. No puede jugar porque se ___ el tobillo.
24. El coche ___ con el árbol.
26. 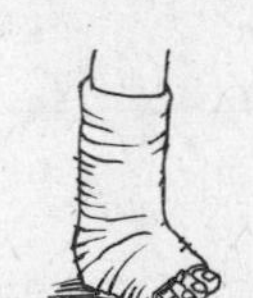 un ___
27. El médico le ___ una inyección.

Vertical

1. La enfermera le puso una ___ por el dolor.
3. una silla de ___
6. *muscles*
7. La niña ___ con un juguete y se cayó.
9. No puedo usar la mano. Me rompí la ___.
11.  Jorgito se cortó la ___.
12. Me ___ mucho la espalda.
13. El médico le dio una ___.
14. El niño se cayó y se ___ mucho.
16. las ___
18. Todavía tiene dolor pero se ___ mejor hoy.
21. Esta mañana Luisa se ___ el dedo con la tijeras.
25. José se cayó y se rompió el ___ de la pierna.

Nombre ______ Hora ______

Fecha ______ Practice Workbook **5B–9**

Organizer

I. Vocabulary

Words for parts of the body | **Words for medical procedures**

Verbs for different types of accidents

II. Grammar

1. Give the preterite forms of these verbs.

decir | **traer**

venir | **poner**

2. Write the present participles of the following verbs:

decir ______ **dormir** ______

pedir ______ **vestir** ______

seguir ______ **creer** ______

Go Online WEB CODE jdd-0517
PHSchool.com

Nombre ______________________ Hora ____________

Fecha ______________________

A ver si recuerdas...

Nos gustan estos programas

Use the cues provided to tell which programs everyone likes or is interested in. Follow the model.

Modelo a Felipe/gustar *Le gustan las comedias.*

1.  a mí / interesar ______________________
____

2.  a mis amigos / encantar ______________________
____

3.  a nosotros / gustar ______________________
____

4. 

a Leonor / interesar ______________________
____

5.  a ti / encantar ______________________
____

6.  a Uds. / gustar ______________________
____

7.  a Pilar y a mí / interesar ______________________
____

8.  a mí / no importar ______________________
____

9.  a Ud. / gustar ______________________
____

Nombre ______________________ Hora ______

Fecha ______________________ Practice Workbook **6A–B**

A ver si recuerdas...

¿Qué hacemos esta noche?

Read the conversation between Sara and José about what they want to do tonight and answer the questions that follow.

SARA: ¿Qué quieres hacer esta noche? ¿Te interesa ver un programa de televisión?

JOSÉ: Vamos a ver qué dan en la televisión. Aquí tengo el periódico. Voy a leer qué programas hay. Bueno, en el canal nueve hay un programa de concursos y en el doce hay un programa de la vida real. ¿Cuál prefieres ver?

SARA: Ninguno de los dos, José. ¿No dan películas esta noche?

JOSÉ: Parece que hay una película policíaca a las ocho. ¿Quieres verla?

SARA: No me gustan las películas violentas. ¿Por qué no vamos al cine? Están dando una película romántica en el centro. Los actores son muy buenos.

JOSÉ: No me gustan las películas románticas. Son tontas. ¿Por qué no vamos a ver una película de ciencia ficción?

SARA: De acuerdo. Me gustan las películas de ciencia ficción. Y están dando una muy interesante aquí.

1. ¿Cómo sabe José qué programas hay en la televisión?

____

2. ¿Qué dan en el canal nueve? ¿Y en el doce?

____

3. ¿Cuál de los dos programas de televisión quiere ver Sara?

____

4. ¿Por qué no quiere ver Sara la película que dan a las ocho?

____

5. ¿Adónde quiere ir Sara?

____

6. ¿Por qué le interesa a Sara la película romántica?

____

7. ¿Cómo son las películas románticas, según José?

____

8. ¿Qué deciden hacer Sara y José por fin?

____

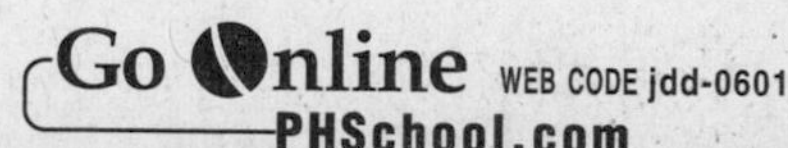

Nombre _______________ Hora _______________

Fecha _______________ Practice Workbook **6A–1**

¿Qué ves?

Complete the sentences below with the correct word or words. Use the illustrations to help you.

1. _______________ anuncia los nombres de los ganadores.

2. A Cecilia le encanta ser _______________ del carnaval.

3. ¡_______________ se vuelven locos!

4. José Alberto ganó _______________. La presentadora le entregó un cheque de un _______________ de pesos.

5. Diez mujeres participan en el _______________ de _______________.

6. _______________ aconseja a los jugadores de su equipo.

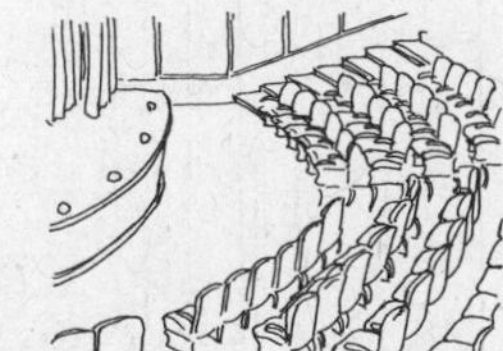

7. El programa de premios es en _______________.

Nombre ______________________ Hora __________

Fecha ______________________ Practice Workbook **6A–2**

¡Mi equipo es mejor!

A. Find out what Pedro and Pablo think about their respective teams by filling in the words to complete their conversation. Each dash represents one letter.

PEDRO: Me pongo muy _ m o _ _ o (_) _ _ o cada vez que mi equipo gana el _ _ m _ _ _ _ n (_) _ _.

PABLO: Y tu equipo lo ganó _ o _ tercera vez el año pasado. Pero este año no van a ser los campeones.

PEDRO: ¿Qué dices, chico? Mi equipo es el mejor de la l _ _ (_). Tiene los mejores jugadores.

PABLO: Bueno, sí *era* el mejor. Pero el equipo mío tiene jugadores fenomenales y al _ _ n _ _ van a ser los campeones de la liga.

PEDRO: Es cierto que tu equipo tiene algunos _ _ l _ _ _ (_) tremendos. Saben jugar muy bien. Pero nuestro entrenador es mejor.

PABLO: Tu equipo _ _ (_) _ _ ó muchos partidos este año. No van a ganar muchos. ¡Y, muchos partidos terminaron en un _ m _ _ (_) _! No es muy bueno.

PEDRO: No importa. Van a ganar el campeonato otra vez. Mi equipo _ o m _ _ _ (_) con más emoción y energía que el equipo tuyo.

PABLO: La _ o m (_) _ _ _ n _ _ _ entre nuestros equipos es siempre muy emocionante. Pero estoy seguro de que mi equipo va a ganar con el _ _ n _ _ o de 5 a 0.

PEDRO: No, mi amigo. ¡Mi equipo va a ganar el campeonato por cuarta vez!

B. Now, unscramble the circled letters to find out the name of the team that won the championship.

L a s _ _ _ _ _ _ _ _

Un partido fenomenal

A. Below is the scrambled story of yesterday's soccer game between the **Lobos** and the **Águilas** (Lobos are in the light-colored jerseys and Águilas are in the dark jerseys). Number the drawings in the order in which they occurred, with **1** being the first event and **8** the last.

____

____

____

____

____

____

____

____

B. Now, tell whether each statement about the game is **cierto** or **falso** by circling the correct answer.

1. Los aficionados se aburrieron en el partido. **cierto** **falso**
2. Mena metió el gol final. **cierto** **falso**
3. Sánchez metió dos goles. **cierto** **falso**
4. El partido terminó en un empate. **cierto** **falso**
5. Los Lobos perdieron. **cierto** **falso**
6. Los aficionados de los dos equipos aplaudieron. **cierto** **falso**
7. Después del partido hubo una entrevista con Sánchez y Mena. **cierto** **falso**

Un artículo en el periódico

Read the following article about the soccer championship, then answer the questions that follow.

Equipo de San Fernando gana el campeonato

En los últimos segundos de un partido emocionante ayer por la tarde, ganó el campeonato del estado el equipo de fútbol de nuestra ciudad. El partido empezó con un gol que metió nuestro jugador Lorenzo Morales, pero unos minutos después metió un gol el jugador Alberto Lamas del equipo de Puerto de Palma y resultó un empate. Todo el mundo creía que así iba a terminar el partido cuando Mauricio Ledesma metió otro gol. El público se volvió loco.

En una entrevista en la televisión, Ledesma le dijo al locutor que cuando metió el gol no lo podía creer. Se sintió alegre y emocionado. Él es ahora el héroe de San Fernando y todo el mundo habla de su gol fenomenal.

1. ¿Qué equipo ganó el campeonato de fútbol?

____

2. ¿En qué momento del partido ganaron?

____

3. ¿Qué hicieron Lorenzo Morales y Alberto Lamas?

____

4. ¿Cuál fue el tanteo durante casi todo el partido?

____

5. ¿Cómo creían todos que iba a terminar el partido?

____

6. ¿Qué hizo el público cuando Ledesma metió el gol?

____

7. ¿Cómo se sintió Ledesma cuando supo que él ganó el campeonato?

____

8. ¿De qué habla todo el mundo en San Fernando?

____

Una noche fenomenal

Marcos and Ana María went out on Saturday night. Use the preterite of the appropriate verb from the box to complete the sentences below about their evening. Follow the model.

servir la comida	**divertirse mucho**
pedir espaguetis	**preferir un restaurante italiano**
reírse mucho	~~**preferir ir al cine**~~
seguir por la calle Miraflores	

Modelo 

Había un concierto muy bueno pero Marcos y Ana María _prefirieron ir al cine_.

1.  Pasaban una comedia y Marcos y Ana María ____________________.

2. 

Después de la película Marcos y Ana María ____________________.

3. 

Marcos ____________________.

4.  Marcos y Ana María ____________________.

5.  El camarero ____________________.

6. Marcos y Ana María ____________________.

Nombre ______ Hora ______

Fecha ______ Practice Workbook **6A–6**

Situaciones diferentes

Complete the following conversations with the preterite of the infinitives in the word bank. Not all of the infinitives will be used. Follow the model.

aburrirse	**~~casarse~~**
divertirse	**dormirse**
lavarse	**ponerse**
cepillarse	**volverse**
sentirse	**enojarse**

Modelo —¿Fuiste a la boda de Bernardo y Lucía?
—Sí, ___se casaron___ el domingo pasado en la iglesia del barrio.

1. —¿No te gustó la película?
   —No, me pareció muy larga y muy poco interesante. Yo ______ mucho.
2. —¿Por qué está enojada la profesora?
   —Ella ______ porque nadie hizo la tarea.
3. —¿Qué le pasó a papá?
   —Papá ______ furioso porque Diego usó el coche y tuvo un accidente.
4. —¿Dónde están los niños?
   —Tenían tanto sueño que ______ a las ocho.
5. —Elena parece muy contenta.
   —Salió con sus amigas y ______ mucho.
6. —No me gusta cuando nos peleamos.
   —De acuerdo. Yo ______ mal la última vez que no nos llevamos bien.
7. —Parece que el público se portó muy mal en el estadio.
   —Sí. Todos ______ locos cuando su equipo perdió el campeonato.
8. —¿Qué hiciste cuando tuviste una cita con Elena?
   —______ la cara y me arreglé el pelo.

Go Online WEB CODE jdd-0605
PHSchool.com

Realidades 2 | Capítulo 6A

Nombre ______ Hora ______

Fecha ______ Practice Workbook **6A–7**

El campeonato

Answer the following questions in complete sentences based on the drawings below.

A.

1. ¿Qué hizo el jugador número once?

______

2. ¿Cómo estuvieron los aficionados? ¿Parece que se aburrieron?

______

3. ¿Cómo se puso el portero (*goalkeeper*)?

______

4. ¿Qué resultó del gol del número once?

______

5. ¿Parece que los jugadores compitieron con emoción? Explica.

______

______

B.

6. ¿Qué ganó el jugador número once?

______

7. ¿Cuál fue el tanteo al final?

______

8. ¿Qué hace el número once ahora?

______

9. ¿Parece que el público se divirtió? Explica.

______

______

Nombre _______________ Hora _______________

Fecha _______________ Practice Workbook **6A–8**

Repaso

Horizontal

1. Cuando Teresa ganó se puso muy ____.
3. Estos atletas son ____. ¡Qué buenos!
5. ¿El ____ final del partido? Cinco a tres.
6. ¿Te ____ furioso porque tu equipo perdió?
7. Este jugador metió un ____.
10. Los aficionados se ____ locos.
11. Vamos a escuchar el ____ del presentador.
15. Alicia ganó el ____ de belleza.
16. Ellos están ____ porque tienen que esperar por mucho tiempo.
18. Yo gané el ____.
19. Raúl se ____ cuando su equipo perdió el partido.
21. Le entregaron un cheque de dos ____ de pesos.
22. El niño se ____ anoche.

Vertical

2. Los aficionados ____.
3. Al ____ del campeonato hablaron los campeones.
4. la ____
8. Los jugadores se enojaron con su ____.
9. ¿Cuál equipo ganó el ____?
11. Ese equipo no ____ en el campeonato este año.
12. Nos ____ mucho porque no pasaba nada.
13. Había mucho público en el ____.
14. El partido terminó en un ____.
17. Nuestro equipo ganó el campeonato por segunda ____.
20. Cada ____ tiene diez equipos.

Nombre ______ Hora ______

Fecha ______ Practice Workbook **6A–9**

Organizer

I. Vocabulary

Words to talk about a sporting event | **Words to talk about a contest**

Verbs used to talk about how you feel

II. Grammar

1. How is the preterite of **-ir** stem-changing verbs different from the preterite of **-er** and **-ar** stem-changing verbs?

2. Give the preterite forms of these verbs.

divertirse | **dormirse**

3. How does Spanish often express the idea of "to get" or "to become?"

Nombre ____________________ Hora ____________

Fecha ____________________ Practice Workbook **6B–1**

¿Quiénes son?

Complete the sentences below with the word or words that correspond to the illustrations.

1. Vimos ____________________ en una película de ciencia ficción.

2. El ____________________ de esta película romántica es muy guapo.

3. Hay cuatro ____________________ principales en esta película.

4. Romeo y Julieta compartieron un ____________________ fuerte.

5. Me gusta el héroe de esta ____________________.

6. Los ____________________ roban el banco.

7. Nos fascina esta ____________________. Es talentosa.

8. Los ____________________ capturan al ____________________.

9. No podían identificar a ____________________.

Go Online WEB CODE jdd-0611
PHSchool.com

Realidades 2 | Nombre ______ | Hora ______

Capítulo 6B | Fecha ______ | Practice Workbook **6B–2**

¿Qué piensan?

Find out what Matilda and Roberto think about some films by completing their conversation with words from your vocabulary. Each dash represents a letter.

MATILDA: Los ___ ___ í ___ ___ ___ ___ ___ dicen que esta película es excelente. Leí un artículo en el periódico.

ROBERTO: Mis amigos me la ___ ___ ___ ___ m ___ ___ ___ d ___ ___ también. Y a mi hermano le f ___ ___ ___ ___ ___ ó .

MATILDA: Yo h ___ ___ ___ ___ t ___ otras películas de este d ___ ___ ___ ___ ___ o ___ . Sus películas tienen buenos ___ ___ g ___ m ___ ___ ___ ___ ___ que no son muy complicados.

ROBERTO: Y los ___ ___ ___ c ___ ___ ___ especiales son muy interesantes.

MATILDA: Parece que Juan Domínguez h ___ ___ ___ ___ l ___ ___ ___ ___ l del detective que busca a unos ladrones. Él es muy buen actor.

ROBERTO: La ___ c ___ ___ ___ c ___ ó ___ es fantástica. Todos los actores deben ganar el premio. Yo vi a los actores en otra película. Tenía un argumento semejante (*similar*), de un detective que ___ r r ___ ___ ___ ___ a un criminal que ___ ___ ___ ó un banco.

MATILDA: Esta película que vamos a ver se ___ r ___ ___ ___ d ___ un crimen y también del amor. Parece que el galán ___ ___ ___ ___ ___ m ___ r ___ d ___ la criminal. Creo que ellos se casan al final.

Una nueva obra de teatro

Marta and Damián are talking about some new theater productions. Complete their conversation with the missing words or phrases.

1. —¿Te gustó la nueva obra de teatro?

   —Sí, mucho. El argumento está ______________________ en uno de mis cuentos favoritos.

2. —A mí me gustó también, pero había demasiada ______________________.

   —Pero sólo mataron a dos personas.

3. —¿La otra nueva obra de teatro fue un éxito?

   —No, fue ______________________. Nadie vino a verla.

4. —No comprendo por qué. Los actores son buenos, ¿verdad?

   —Sí, el hombre que hace ______________________ del padre fue muy bueno.

5. —¿Quién fue? ¿Antonio Rivera?

   —Sí, él es un actor que siempre tiene ______________________. Todas sus películas son buenas.

6. —¿Y la obra es interesante?

   —A mí me parece que sí. Tiene ______________________ muy emocionante. Pero es un poco complicado.

7. —La obra trata de un crimen, ¿no?

   —Sí, un ladrón ______________________ una casa y ______________________ a la familia que vive en la casa. Es un poco triste.

8. —¿Y qué pasa al final?

   —La policía ________________ al ladrón y lo arresta.

Go Online WEB CODE jdd-0612
PHSchool.com

El crimen

Look at the picture below of a "Hollywood" robbery scene that is being filmed for a new movie. Study the scene and answer the questions that follow.

1. ¿De qué se trata esta escena?

2. ¿Quiénes son los personajes principales?

3. ¿Cuál es el argumento?

4. ¿Hay violencia en la escena? Explica.

5. ¿Hay víctimas aquí? ¿De qué son víctimas?

6. ¿Cómo crees que va a terminar esta película? ¿Van a ganar los malos o van a ganar los buenos? Explica.

El por qué de las cosas

Why do the people below feel the way they do? Using phrases from the word bank, write a complete sentence to explain each statement. Follow the model.

molestar mucho/los mosquitos	**quedar mal/la falda que tiene**
no gustar/la violencia	**doler/un diente**
encantar/los postres	**interesar/la historia**
fascinar/las películas	**parecer triste/el argumento**
~~aburrir/la ciencia ficción~~	

Modelo Pedro no quiere ver la película sobre los extraterrestres.
Le aburre la ciencia ficción.

1. Los niños quieren más helado.
____.
2. Yo tengo que ir a ver al dentista.
____.
3. Nosotros queremos estudiar las ciudades antiguas.
____.
4. María tiene que comprar otra falda.
____.
5. Todos lloran cuando ven esa película.
____.
6. José no quiere ver la película policíaca porque muere mucha gente.
____.
7. Consuelo va al cine dos veces por semana.
____.
8. Tratas de matar ese mosquito.
____.

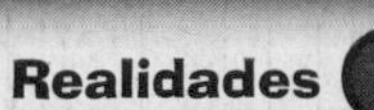

Realidades 2

Capítulo 6B

Nombre ______________________ Hora ________

Fecha ______________________ Practice Workbook **6B–6**

Empieza la fiesta

Carolina is in charge of tonight's surprise party. She is checking to make sure that everything has been done. Answer each of her questions in a complete sentence. Follow the model.

Modelo ¿Quién va a alquilar la película? (José)

José ya la ha alquilado.

1. ¿Quién va a pedir la pizza? (Margarita y yo)

   ____.

2. ¿Quién va a hacer las galletas? (Isabel)

   ____.

3. ¿Quién va a traer los refrescos? (Luis y Paco)

   ____.

4. ¿Quién va a poner la mesa? (yo)

   ____.

5. ¿Quién va a llamar a Luisa? (Francisco)

   ____.

6. ¿Quién va a escoger la música? (nosotros)

   ____.

7. ¿Quién va a romper la piñata? (Carlos)

   ____.

8. ¿Quién va a arreglar la sala? (Marta)

   ____.

Realidades 2 Nombre ____ Hora ____

Capítulo 6B Fecha ____ Practice Workbook **6B–7**

¿Cómo se escribe?

Order each group of words into a logical sentence using the present perfect. Follow the model.

Modelo el criminal / arrestar / el detective / a

El detective ha arrestado al criminal.

1. tener que / el examen / Jesús / para / estudiar

   ____.

2. una película policíaca / yo / ver

   ____.

3. le / escribir / Javier / esta semana / a Sarita

   ____.

4. los ladrones / la casa / robar / el dinero / de

   ____.

5. la tienda / de / nosotros / alquilar / un video

   ____.

6. comentarios / la crítica / la película / sobre / hacer

   ____.

7. capturar / la policía / los criminales / a

   ____.

8. recomendar / Pilar / me / una película romántica

   ____.

9. tratar de / Linda / matar / el mosquito

   ____.

10. el mosquito / de Juan / bajar en / el libro

    ____.

Repaso

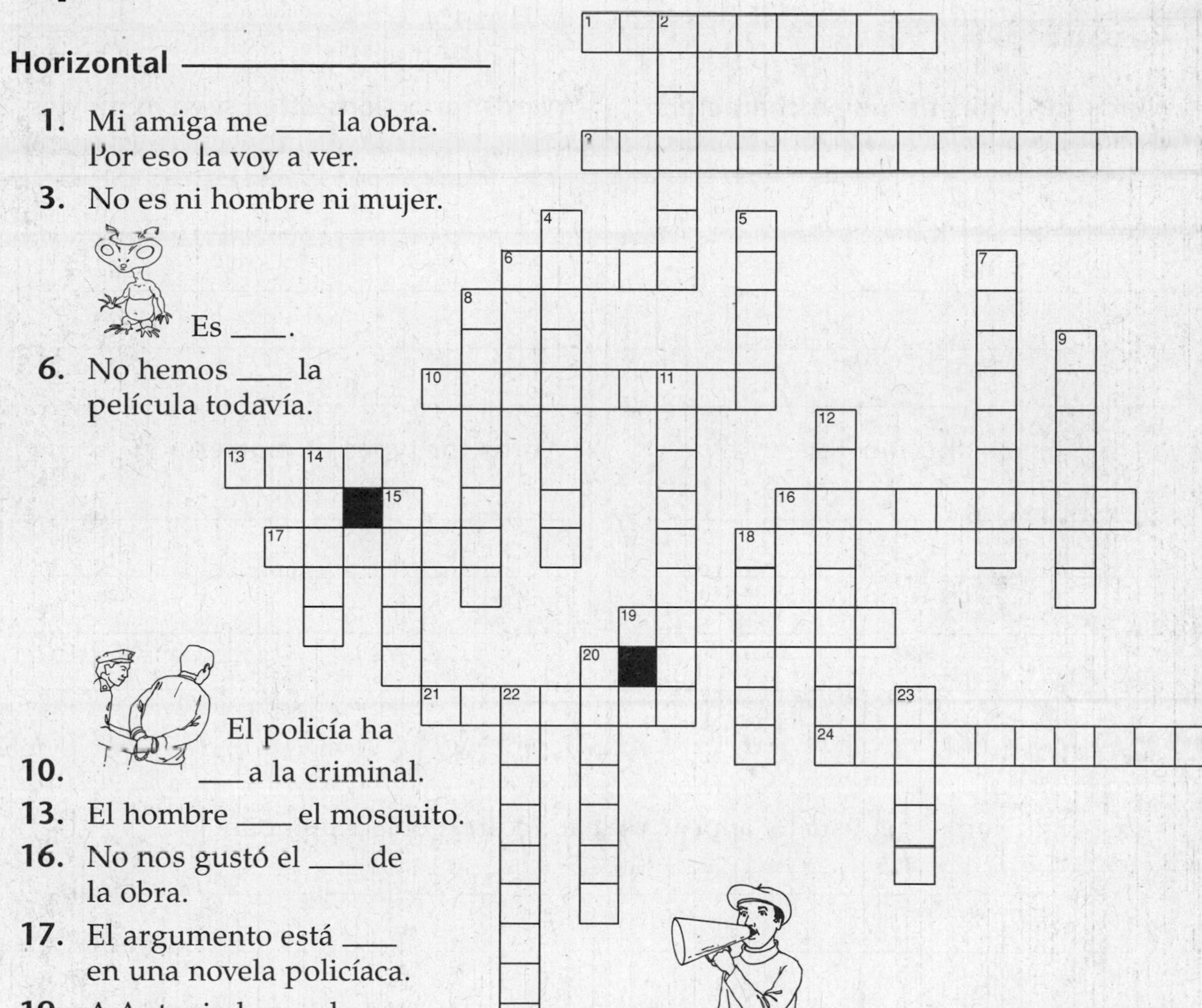

Horizontal

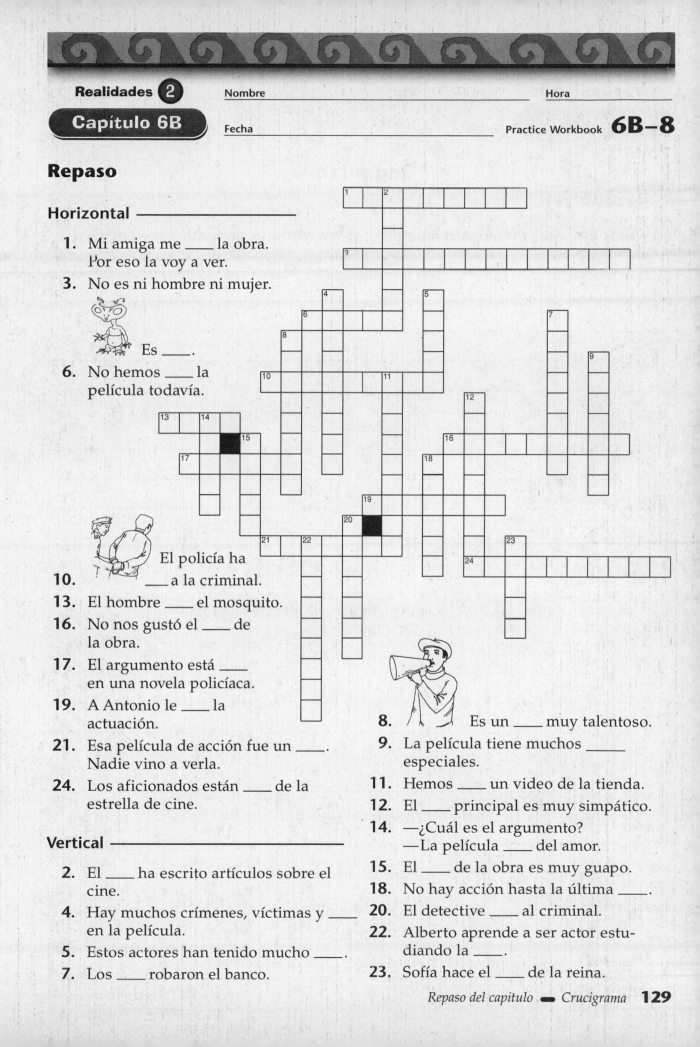

1. Mi amiga me ____ la obra. Por eso la voy a ver.
3. No es ni hombre ni mujer. Es ____.
6. No hemos ____ la película todavía.
10. El policía ha ____ a la criminal.
13. El hombre ____ el mosquito.
16. No nos gustó el ____ de la obra.
17. El argumento está ____ en una novela policíaca.
19. A Antonio le ____ la actuación.
21. Esa película de acción fue un ____. Nadie vino a verla.
24. Los aficionados están ____ de la estrella de cine.

Vertical

2. El ____ ha escrito artículos sobre el cine.
4. Hay muchos crímenes, víctimas y ____ en la película.
5. Estos actores han tenido mucho ____.
7. Los ____ robaron el banco.
8. Es un ____ muy talentoso.
9. La película tiene muchos ____ especiales.
11. Hemos ____ un video de la tienda.
12. El ____ principal es muy simpático.
14. —¿Cuál es el argumento?
—La película ____ del amor.
15. El ____ de la obra es muy guapo.
18. No hay acción hasta la última ____.
20. El detective ____ al criminal.
22. Alberto aprende a ser actor estudiando la ____.
23. Sofía hace el ____ de la reina.

Nombre ______________________ Hora __________

Fecha ______________________ Practice Workbook **6B–9**

Organizer

I. Vocabulary

Words for types of movie characters

____

____

____

____

____

Words for actions often seen in movies

____

____

____

____

____

Words for making movies

____

____

____

____

Words for types of movies

____

____

____

____

II. Grammar

1. List eight verbs that usually appear with an indirect object pronoun.

________________ ________________

________________ ________________

________________ ________________

________________ ________________

2. How is the present perfect tense formed?

____

3. Where are object pronouns placed in the present perfect?

____

4. What are the past participles of the following verbs?

decir	________	**hacer**	________	**romper**	________
devolver	________	**morir**	________	**ver**	________
escribir	________	**poner**	________	**volver**	________

Realidades 2 | Nombre ______ | Hora ______

Capítulo 7A | Fecha ______ | Practice Workbook **7A–A**

A ver si recuerdas...

Me encanta comer

Your teacher is taking a survey on what your classmates eat and how they prepare for meals. Use the cues provided to complete each person's response. Follow the model.

Modelo yo / venir ___Vengo___ a la cafetería para comer el almuerzo.

1. yo / conocer ____________ una buena tienda de frutas.
2. yo / hacer ____________ bistec y espaguetis hoy.
3. yo / mantener ____________ la salud comiendo ensalada.
4. yo / decir ____________ que el pescado es bueno para la salud.
5. yo / poner ____________ la mesa antes de preparar la cena.
6. yo / salir ____________ a cenar a las ocho cuando voy a un restaurante elegante.
7. yo / ofrecerle ____________ unas fresas a mi amiga cuando las tengo.
8. yo / tener ____________ hambre hoy, y quiero comer papas fritas.
9. yo / oír ____________ las noticias sobre cómo mantener la salud, y voy a comer más frutas.
10. yo / obedecer ____________ a mis padres cuando dicen que debo comer mis verduras.

Nombre ______________________ Hora ____________

Fecha ______________________ Practice Workbook **7A–B**

A ver si recuerdas...

¡Nos gusta comer!

The illustrations below represent people's health regimens. Identify each item and write what each person does in the spaces provided. Follow the model.

Modelo Yo *hago un pollo* para ser saludable.

1. Paco y Alberto ______________________ todos los días por la mañana.
2. Guillermo ______________________ comiendo bien y levantando pesas.
3. Yo ______________________ dos horas cada día.
4. Los estudiantes ______________________ ocho vasos de ______________________ todos los días.
5. Anita ______________________ cada día.
6. Alonso ______________________ tres veces a la semana.
7. Paquita ______________________ porque es bueno para la salud.

Go Online WEB CODE jdd-0701
PHSchool.com

¿Qué hay en tu cocina?

Complete the following sentences based on the drawings.

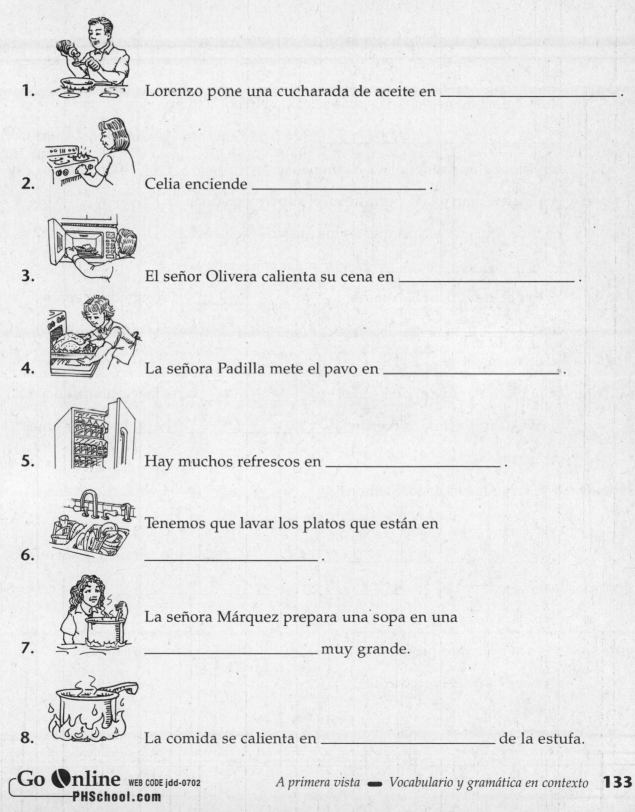

1.  Lorenzo pone una cucharada de aceite en ____________________.

2.  Celia enciende ____________________.

3.  El señor Olivera calienta su cena en ____________________.

4.  La señora Padilla mete el pavo en ____________________.

5.  Hay muchos refrescos en ____________________.

6.  Tenemos que lavar los platos que están en ____________________.

7.  La señora Márquez prepara una sopa en una ____________________ muy grande.

8. La comida se calienta en ____________________ de la estufa.

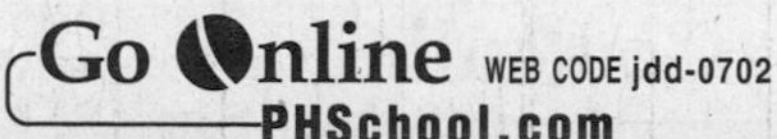

WEB CODE jdd-0702

Nombre ____________________ Hora ____________

Fecha ____________________ Practice Workbook **7A–2**

Nuestra comida sabrosa

Find out what Regina and Sandra are cooking for dinner tonight by completing their conversation. Each dash represents a letter.

REGINA: Sandra, prueba el caldo, por favor. ¿Necesito ___ ñ ___ ___ ___ ___ más sal?

SANDRA: No, Regina, no necesitamos más sal. Está bueno. Yo hiervo los ___ a ___ a ___ ___ ___ ___ ___ ahora. ¡Me encantan los mariscos! Vamos a servirlos como primer plato. Ya preparé la s ___ l ___ ___. Tiene mucho ajo.

REGINA: ¿La hiciste aquí o la compraste en el supermercado?

SANDRA: La hice aquí en casa porque no me gustan las salsas ___ ___ ___ a ___ a ___ a ___ ni las congeladas.

REGINA: Yo también prefiero la comida ___ r ___ ___ ___ ___. La comida preparada con i ___ ___ ___ ___ ___ i ___ ___ ___ ___ s frescos como los tomates y el ajo es mejor.

SANDRA: Muy bien. Yo puse el pollo en el ___ ___ ___ n ___ a cocinar y ahora enciendo el fuego en la estufa. Necesito c ___ ___ ___ n ___ ___ ___ las papas antes de servirlas.

REGINA: Y yo hago la ensalada. Siempre m ___ ___ ___ ___ o el vinagre con el ___ c ___ ___ ___ e. Es sabroso. Quizás añado una ___ ___ ___ h ___ ___ ___ d ___ de ___ ___ o picado también. ¡Qué bueno!

SANDRA: Saco el postre del ___ e f ___ ___ g e ___ ___ ___ o ___ y todo está listo para comer.

REGINA: ¡Por fin podemos probar esta ___ ___ c ___ t ___ tan sabrosa! Tiene muchos buenos ingredientes.

Go Online WEB CODE jdd-0702 PHSchool.com

En la cocina

Mrs. Benítez is showing her daughter Magali how to get a meal ready for company. Complete what she tells Magali with the correct form of the appropriate word.

1. Si no te gusta la sopa, debes ______________ más sal.
2. Saca los platos, los tenedores, los cuchillos y las cucharas. Tienes que ______________ la mesa para ocho personas.
3. No ______________ de los vasos. Son tan necesarios como los platos.
4. No debes usar pedazos de ajo tan grandes. Hay que ______________los.
5. Hay que ______________ el horno para poder cocinar la carne.
6. Debes ______________ la carne en el horno por dos horas.
7. ______________ la carne con papas fritas y legumbres.
8. Tienes que ______________las papas primero. Debes ______________las sin la piel (*skin*).
9. Dejaste el fuego encendido (*lit*) en la estufa. Debes ______________lo.
10. Necesitamos ______________ todos los ingredientes para hacer la salsa.
11. Vamos a poner el agua en la olla. Debemos ______________la para tener una salsa caliente.
12. Tienes que ______________ la salsa a menudo para ver si necesita más sal o pimienta.

Nombre ______________________ Hora ______________

Fecha ______________________ Practice Workbook **7A–4**

Preparando comida

Answer the following questions in complete sentences based on the drawings.

1. ¿Qué hace Marta con la sopa? ____ .

2. ¿Qué hace José con el ajo? ____ .

3. ¿Cómo está el café? ____ .

4. ¿Cómo se hace el arroz? ____ .

5. ¿Qué hace Marcos? ____ .

6. ¿Qué hizo Felipe con el aceite? ____ .

7. ¿Qué va a hacer María con el ajo? ____ .

8. ¿Con qué se sirve la paella? ____ .

Go Online WEB CODE jdd-0703
PHSchool.com

¡Qué mal cocinero!

Mrs. Bermúdez is giving her son Pablo advice about cooking. Everything he thinks he should do, he shouldn't. Write her answers to Pablo's questions using **tú** commands. Follow the model.

Modelo ¿Debo apagar el horno? (la estufa)
No, no lo apagues. Apaga la estufa.

1. ¿Debo picar el arroz? (los ajos)
   ____________________.
2. ¿Debo tirar la leche? (el agua)
   ____________________.
3. ¿Debo poner el arroz en el microondas? (en la olla)
   ____________________.
4. ¿Debo pelar los tomates? (las papas)
   ____________________.
5. ¿Debo hacer los espaguetis? (los huevos)
   ____________________.
6. ¿Debo freír la ensalada? (el pollo)
   ____________________.
7. ¿Debo cortar la lechuga? (las cebollas)
   ____________________.
8. ¿Debo añadir azúcar a la paella? (sal)
   ____________________.
9. ¿Debo mezclar el aceite con los tomates? (el vinagre)
   ____________________.
10. ¿Debo hervir los huevos en la sartén? (la olla)
    ____________________.

Enseñando a cocinar

Answer your friend's questions about cooking using the impersonal **se** and the cues provided. Follow the model.

Modelo ¿Qué hago para preparar este plato? (picar / ajos)

Se pican los ajos para preparar este plato.

1. ¿Qué debo comprar para hacer una paella? (usar / muchos mariscos)

   ____________________ para hacer una paella.

2. ¿Qué comen Uds. con la paella? (servir / una ensalada)

   ____________________ con la paella.

3. ¿Cómo cocinamos el pollo? (poner / en el horno)

   ____________________ el pollo

   ____________________.

4. ¿Qué pongo en el caldo? (añadir / sal)

   ____________________ al caldo.

5. ¿Para este plato compramos ingredientes frescos? (usar / comida enlatada) Sí, no

   ____________________.

6. ¿Cómo hacemos la paella? (preparar / en la sartén)

   ____________________ la paella

   ____________________.

7. ¿Qué haces con las legumbres congeladas? (calentar / en el microondas)

   ____________________ las legumbres congeladas

   ____________________.

8. ¿Y los huevos? (batir / los huevos)

   ____________________ para esta receta.

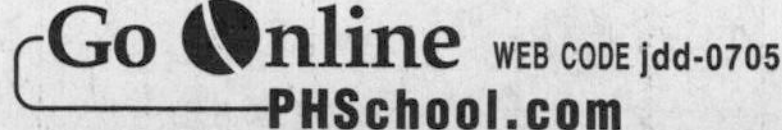

Cocinando juntos

Create dialogues between two friends working in the kitchen. One friend asks a question using the impersonal **se**, the other responds with a negative **tú** command. Replace any direct object nouns by the corresponding pronouns.

Modelo añadir la sal ahora

—¿*Se añade la sal ahora*?

—*No, no la añadas ahora*.

1. calentar la salsa

—¿______________________________?

—______________________________.

2. freír los ajos

—¿______________________________?

—______________________________.

3. encender la estufa

—¿______________________________?

—______________________________.

4. dejar la olla en la estufa

—¿______________________________?

—______________________________.

5. mezclar los ingredientes

—¿______________________________?

—______________________________.

6. batir los huevos

—¿______________________________?

—______________________________.

7. pelar los tomates

—¿______________________________?

—______________________________.

8. apagar la estufa

—¿______________________________?

—______________________________.

Repaso

Horizontal

1. el ___ de oliva
5. *Turn on.*
7. Nos encantan las frutas y las verduras ___.
8. El agua ya ___. Echa el arroz.
10. Según la receta, se añade una ___ de vinagre.
12. Me encanta la paella, especialmente los ___.
16. el ___
17. ___ (tú) los huevos bien antes de freírlos.
18. la ___
19. No te ___ de apagar el fuego.
20. Se puede freír en la ___.
21. Esta receta tiene muchos ___.

Vertical

2. No ___ (tú) el aceite. Lo vas a necesitar.
3. No ___ (tú) el ajo con ese cuchillo.
4. No ___ (tú) las papas todavía.
5. La comida es ___.
6. ___ (tú) la salsa y dime si necesita más sal.
9. Se sirve el bistec con papas ___.
10. No se puede preparar la carne porque está todavía ___.
11. Saca el queso del ___.
12. Calienta la comida en el ___.
13. Enciende el fuego y ___ el caldo.
14. Pon el plato en el ___ y déjalo por dos horas.
15. Corta el ajo en ___ pequeños.

Nombre ____________ Hora ____________

Fecha ____________ Practice Workbook **7A–9**

Organizer

I. Vocabulary

Words for food

____
____
____
____
____

Words for items in the kitchen

____
____
____
____
____

Verbs for food preparation

____
____
____
____
____

Other words to talk about cooking

____
____
____
____
____

II. Grammar

1. To form negative **tú** commands, drop the letter ____ from the present-tense ____ form and add the letters ____ for **-ar** verbs and the letters ____ for **-er** and **-ir** verbs.
2. Give the negative **tú** command for these verbs.

hablar	no __________	**ofrecer**	no __________	**buscar**	no __________
ir	no __________	**dar**	no __________	**empezar**	no __________
ser	no __________	**estar**	no __________	**decir**	no __________

3. What does the impersonal **se** signify?

____

4. What form of the verb is used in the impersonal **se** construction?

____

WEB CODE jdd-0707

Realidades 2 | Nombre ____ | Hora ____

Capítulo 7B | Fecha ____ | Practice Workbook **7B–1**

Un picnic normal

Complete the following sentences with the vocabulary word suggested by the picture.

1. Hay muchas ______________________ en el cielo.
2. Es difícil andar por este sendero porque tiene muchas ______________________ .
3. Las ______________________ les molestan a los chicos.
4. ¡Las ______________________ están comiendo el pan que trajimos!
5. María Luisa trae ______________________ para hacer un fuego.
6. Rafael ha sacado un ________________ para encender la fogata.
7. Micaela prepara la carne en la ______________________ .
8. Antonio pone ______________________ en su carne.
9. También hay ______________________ para el almuerzo.

Go Online WEB CODE jdd-0711
PHSchool.com

¡Qué bien comer afuera!

The Estévez and Fernández families are getting together in the backyard for a barbecue. Write what each person does at the reunion in the space provided. Follow the model.

Modelo Lupe y Paco *comen al aire libre*.

1. Daniel ______________________.
2. Regina ______________________.
3. Papá ______________________.
4. La madre va a ______________________.
5. La señora Fernández ______________________.
6. Graciela y Lucía ______________________.
7. La familia Estévez ______________________.

Nombre ______ Hora ______

Fecha ______ Practice Workbook **7B–3**

Un picnic horrible

The Ramos family went on a picnic this weekend, but it did not go well. Answer the following questions in complete sentences based on the drawings.

Modelo 
¿Por qué no hicieron el picnic allí?
No hicieron el picnic allí porque el suelo estaba mojado .

1. ¿Por qué no comieron en el picnic? ______
______.

2. ¿Por qué no asaron las chuletas? ______
______.

3. ¿Qué no trajo la hermana? ______
______.

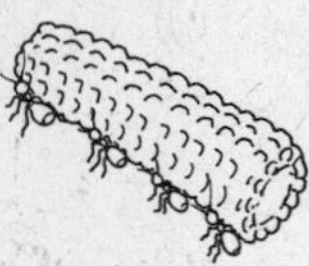
4. ¿Qué se llevaron las hormigas? ______
______.

5. ¿Qué se le olvidó a Enrique para hacer el guacamole? ______
______.

6. ¿Por qué Angélica no pudo encender la parrilla? ______
______.

7. ¿Por qué Esteban no quiso comer la tortilla? ______
______.

¡Qué parrillada!

Read the conversation between Mr. Rubio and his students at their class barbecue. Then, answer the questions that follow in complete sentences.

SR. RUBIO: Muchachos, den una caminata en este sendero pero tengan cuidado.

PABLO: Señor Rubio, yo no quiero caminar más. Tengo hambre. ¿Cuándo vamos a comer?

SR. RUBIO: Vamos a hacer la parrillada muy pronto. El señor Salinas está haciendo la fogata. Coman cerezas o duraznos mientras esperan.

MARCOS: Pero yo prefiero comer carne asada con frijoles.

SR. RUBIO: Entiendo, Marcos, pero la fogata no está todavía. ¿Por qué no traen más leña? Y luego abran la cesta y saquen la carne. Pero no pongan la comida en el suelo porque hay hormigas por todas partes.

PABLO: (*sacando comida*) Aquí tiene Ud. mayonesa, maíz, cerezas…

MARCOS: …duraznos, salsa de tomate, mostaza y nada más.

SR. RUBIO: No puede ser. ¿Dónde está la carne de res?

PABLO: No queda nada dentro, señor. Creo que Ud. se olvidó de traerla.

SR. RUBIO: Lo siento, chicos. ¡Hagan ahora unos sándwiches de mayonesa y mostaza! No tenemos que esperar.

1. ¿Por qué no quiere Pablo dar una caminata?

____

2. ¿Quién hace la fogata?

____

3. ¿Para qué es la fogata?

____

4. ¿Qué quiere comer Marcos?

____

5. ¿Por qué no deben poner la comida en el suelo?

____

6. ¿Qué hay en la cesta?

____

7. ¿Por qué no van a comer carne?

____

8. ¿Qué van a comer?

____

Realidades 2

Capítulo 7B

Nombre ______ Hora ______

Fecha ______ Practice Workbook **7B–5**

Cómo hacer una buena parrillada

Mr. Álvarez has a lot of questions about camping. What advice can you give him? Use the drawings and the verbs given to help you. Use **Ud.** and **Uds.** commands in your answers.

Modelo

(poner) ¿Qué debo hacer con las cestas?

Póngalas en la mesa.

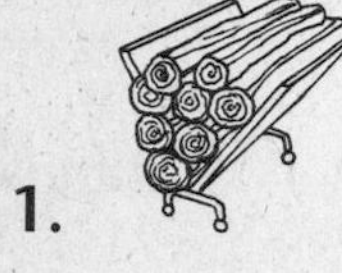

1. (traer) ¿Qué necesitamos hacer ahora para encender el fuego? ______

2. (ir) ¿Dónde podemos encontrarla? ______

3. (buscar) ¿Qué clase de lugar es bueno para la fogata? ______

4. (no dejar) ¿Dónde debo poner los fósforos? ______

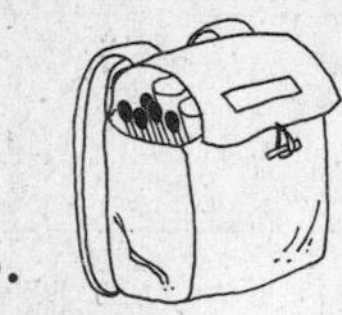

5. (sacar) ¿Qué necesitamos ahora? ______

6. (no olvidarse) Creo que lo tengo todo. ______

7. (cortar) ¿Qué debemos hacer con las chuletas? ______

8. (servir) ¿Con qué debemos servir las chuletas? ______

Go Online WEB CODE jdd-0713 PHSchool.com

Por allí

A. Indicate why **por** is used in each of the following cases. Choose the letter of the reason from the box.

> **a.** **to indicate length of time or distance**
> **b.** **to indicate movement through, along, or around**
> **c.** **to indicate an exchange of one thing for another**
> **d.** **to indicate reason or motive**
> **e.** **to indicate a substitution or action on someone's behalf**
> **f.** **to indicate means of transportation or communication**

1. _____ Este lugar no es bueno por estar demasiado mojado.
2. _____ Hay que cocinar la sopa por una hora.
3. _____ Te doy mis papas fritas por tu sándwich.
4. _____ Yo puedo jugar por ti si no puedes ir al partido.
5. _____ Caminamos por el bosque buscando leña.
6. _____ Viajamos por tres horas en coche.
7. _____ ¿Por qué no nos hablamos por teléfono?

B. Complete the following conversation with the **por** where necessary. If **por** is not required, mark the blank with an **X**. The first one has been done for you.

MARTÍN: Me gustaría (1) ____X____ hacer una parrillada.

PABLO: A mí también. Hoy (2) ___________ la tarde la podemos hacer. Yo tengo chuletas de cerdo. ¿Te gustan?

MARTÍN: (3) ___________ lo general prefiero la carne de res, pero el cerdo también me gusta. ¿Dónde compraste (4) ___________ la carne? ¿Costó mucho?

PABLO: No, pagué (5) ___________ diez dólares (6) ___________ cuatro chuletas.

MARTÍN: Vamos a caminar (7) ___________ el sendero del bosque hasta encontrar un lugar seco. Allí haremos la fogata.

PABLO: Creo que las chuletas se cocinan (8) ___________ unos veinte minutos.

MARTÍN: ¿Quieres papas también?

PABLO: Sí, (9) ___________ supuesto.

MARTÍN: Entonces yo voy a comprar papas. Y refrescos también.

PABLO: Muy bien. Y trae fósforos también, (10)___________ favor.

Niños, ¡hagan lo que digo!

Ángela and Ramón are going camping for the first time. Their father gives them advice. Use **Uds.** commands to find out what he tells them, then combine the elements to write complete sentences. Use **por** when necessary.

Modelo levantarse temprano / la mañana
Levántense temprano por la mañana.

1. ir al campo / tren
____
2. comprar los boletos / cinco dólares
____
3. viajar / una hora
____
4. buscar un lugar / el lago
____
5. caminar / el sendero del bosque
____
6. andar / el bosque para buscar leña
____
7. comer / la tienda de campaña
____
8. encender la fogata / la tarde
____
9. charlar / la fogata
____

Repaso

Horizontal

1. ____ (Ud.) la carne a la parrilla.
4. ____ (Ud.) la tortilla de maíz.
6. Prepare el guacamole con estos ____.
9. Niños, ¡no ____ con los fósforos!
11. ¡Qué cerezas más ____!
12. Se pueden ver muchas ____ hoy.
15. Nos encanta la carne ____.
17. Estamos muy ____.
18. ____ Uds. más leña para la fogata.
20. Compre ____ para hacer el pan.
21. ____ Uds. frijoles con la carne.
23. ____ (Ud.) cuidado por los mosquitos.

Vertical

2. No ____ (Ud.) de la casa.
3. No ____ (Uds.) por ese sendero.
5. ¡Cuánto nos molestan las ____!
7. Se venden duraznos en este ____.
8. Deje sus zapatos sucios ____ de la casa.
10. No ponga la cesta en el ____.
13. La salsa tiene un ____ muy rico.
14. No ____ (Uds.) la parrillada aquí porque hay hormigas.
16. ____ (Uds.) una caminata por el bosque.
19. Esta carne de res es muy ____.
22. Señora, ____ (Ud.) las chuletas a la parrilla.

Nombre ____________ Hora ____________

Fecha ____________ Practice Workbook **7B–9**

Organizer

I. Vocabulary

Words for picnic foods

____

____

____

____

____

Words describing foods and the outdoors

____

____

____

____

____

Verbs to talk about the outdoors

____

____

____

____

____

Words to talk about eating outdoors

____

____

____

____

____

II. Grammar

1. To form **Ud.** and **Uds.** commands, use the present-tense _____ form. Then, add the letter _____ or the letters _____ for **-ar** verbs and the letter _____ or the letters _____ for **-er** and **-ir** verbs.
2. What spelling changes take place in **Ud.** and **Uds.** commands in verbs ending in **-car**, **-gar**, and **-zar**?

   ____

3. Give the **Ud.** command form for these verbs:

   dar __________ **ir** __________ **ser** __________ **hacer** __________

4. List four uses of **por**.

   ____

   ____

   ____

   ____

Nombre ______ Hora ______

Fecha ______ Practice Workbook **8A–A**

Hablando de las vacaciones

Complete the sentences below to find out what everyone did while on vacation. Use the scrambled words to help you.

Modelo Yo esquié en las *montañas* (ñnamtosa).

1. Lisa y Paco fueron de compras al ______ (doremac) al aire libre.
2. Jorge y Elena nadaron en la ______ (cinapsi) del hotel.
3. Fui al ______ (ripadot) final de la liga profesional de fútbol español.
4. Ud. visitó las ______ (seducadi) famosas de Europa, como Barcelona.
5. Tú fuiste al ______ (datosie) para ver el partido conmigo.
6. Inés y sus amigos fueron a la ______ (apayl) para tomar el sol.
7. Los Ramos fueron de cámping en el ______ (pocma) cerca de un ______ (goal).
8. El verano pasado fuimos de ______ (conesaciva) a las montañas.
9. ¿Conoces tú un buen ______ (rugal) para bucear?
10. Los Pacheco vieron una ______ (brao) de ______ (arttoe) en Nueva York.
11. Ignacio visitó varios ______ (spuqaer) de ______ (risevoseind).
12. Los Chacón visitaron el ______ (urapeq) ______ (alincona) de Colorado.

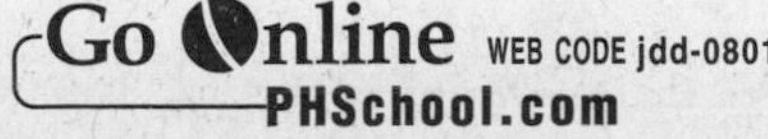

WEB CODE jdd-0801

Realidades 1 | Nombre ____________ | Hora ____________

Capítulo 8A | Fecha ____________ | Practice Workbook **8A–B**

A ver si recuerdas...

¡Nos gusta ir de vacaciones!

Use the elements given to tell what people like, want, and are going to do on vacation.

Modelo Osvaldo (gustar)
A Osvaldo le gusta ir de pesca.

1. Tú (encantar) ____
____.

2. Yo (ir a) ____
____.

3. Alejandro y Laura (preferir) ____
____.

4. Ud. (desear) ____
____.

5. Uds. (gustar) ____
____.

6. Federico (querer) ____
____.

7. Nosotros (deber) ____
____.

8. Irene (pensar) ____
____.

Go Online WEB CODE jdd-0801 PHSchool.com

Viajando en avión

Look at each drawing below, and write the words that best complete the sentence to describe it.

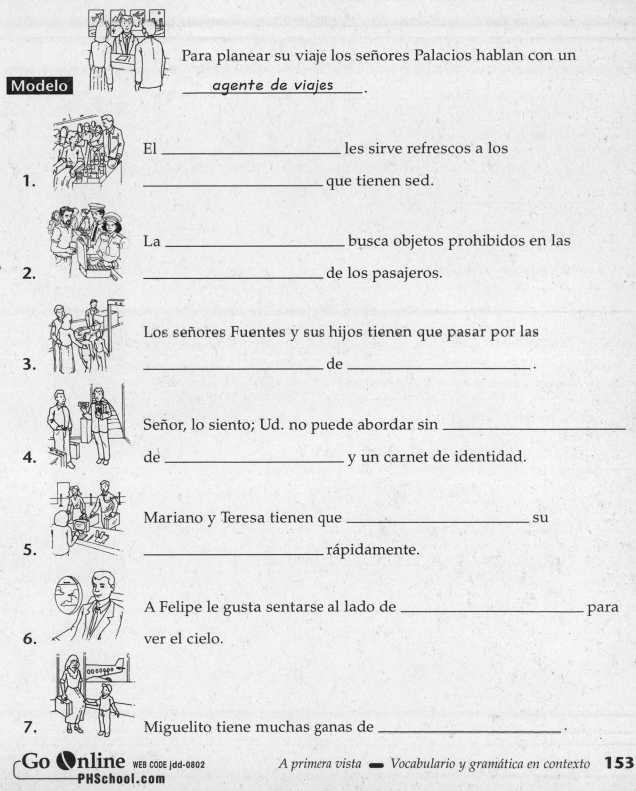

Modelo Para planear su viaje los señores Palacios hablan con un *agente de viajes*.

1. El ______________ les sirve refrescos a los ______________ que tienen sed.

2. La ______________ busca objetos prohibidos en las ______________ de los pasajeros.

3. Los señores Fuentes y sus hijos tienen que pasar por las ______________ de ______________.

4. Señor, lo siento; Ud. no puede abordar sin ______________ de ______________ y un carnet de identidad.

5. Mariano y Teresa tienen que ______________ su ______________ rápidamente.

6. A Felipe le gusta sentarse al lado de ______________ para ver el cielo.

7. Miguelito tiene muchas ganas de ______________.

Problemas y soluciones

Complete each mini-conversation about traveling in a logical manner.

Modelo —¿Por qué tienes tanta prisa?

—Porque no hice una *reservación* y casi es hora de salir.

1. —Quiero ir de Nueva York a Caracas, pero sin hacer escala.

   —Voy a ver si hay un ______________________ entonces.

2. —¡Hasta luego, mi hija!

   —No tenemos que despedirnos aquí, mamá. Podemos esperar hasta la puerta

   ______________________.

3. —¿Nuestro avión no ha llegado todavía?

   —No, hay un pequeño ______________________.

4. —¿Por qué siempre hacemos escala en este aeropuerto?

   —Porque esta ______________________ tiene todos sus aviones aquí.

5. —Nuestro vuelo es el 368, ¿verdad?

   —Sí, el vuelo 368 con ______________________ a Acapulco.

6. —¿De dónde sale el vuelo número 455?

   —De la puerta número 20. ¿No oíste el ______________________?

7. —¿Dónde está tu equipaje?

   —Están ______________________lo ahora.

Los viajes

Use the drawings below to answer the questions in complete sentences.

Modelo

¿Está abierta o cerrada la agencia de viajes?

La agencia de viajes está abierta.

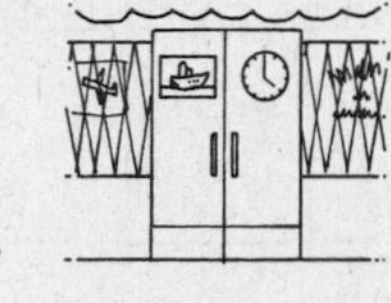

1. ¿Por qué no hay agentes en la agencia de viajes a las tres de la tarde?
______________________________.

2. ¿Qué pasó con el tren de las cuatro?
______________________________.

3. ¿Cuánto dura el viaje en tren desde Madrid a París?
______________________________.

4. ¿Qué pasa en la puerta de embarque?
______________________________.

5. ¿Quién aborda primero?
______________________________.

6. ¿Por qué el pasajero no puede pasar por la aduana?
______________________________.

7. ¿Hay muchos turistas en el aeropuerto? ¿Parecen extranjeros o no? ¿Por qué? ______________________________
______________________________.

Nombre ____ Hora ____

Fecha ____ Practice Workbook **8A–4**

¿De quién se habla?

Read the following situations and answer the questions in complete sentences in the spaces provided.

1. Isabel pasa por las inspecciones de seguridad con los auxiliares de vuelo. Ella es la primera que aborda el avión. ¿Quién es ella?

   ____

2. Rafael quiere hacer un viaje a Cancún. Planea un viaje de una semana porque tiene que volver al trabajo. ¿Qué tipo de boleto debe comprar?

   ____

3. Los auxiliares me saludan: "¡Bienvenido a nuestra línea aérea, señor! ¿Tiene Ud. la tarjeta de embarque?" Paso por la puerta de embarque y abordo el avión. Tengo un asiento de ventanilla. ¿Quién soy?

   ____

4. Sofía salió en avión de Chicago a las tres de la tarde. El vuelo duró dos horas y media. Llegó a San Francisco a las ocho de la noche. ¿Fue un vuelo directo o hizo escala?

   ____

5. José espera a su amigo que viene en avión desde Colombia. José sabe que su amigo debe pasar primero por la inspección de seguridad. ¿Por dónde tiene que pasar su amigo después?

   ____

6. "Tengo mi pasaporte y mi tarjeta de embarque. Es mi primer viaje a un país extranjero. Tengo muchas ganas de visitar muchos museos." ¿Para qué está lista esta turista?

   ____

7. "¡Uf! Primero esperé en la inspección de seguridad. Luego me dijeron que mi vuelo llega con retraso. Y ahora anuncian que el vuelo tiene problemas mecánicos. ¡Caramba!" ¿Qué necesita tener este pasajero?

   ____

Go Online WEB CODE jdd-0803
PHSchool.com

Realidades 2 Nombre ____ Hora ____

Capítulo 8A Fecha ____ Practice Workbook **8A–5**

Ud. es agente de viajes

Answer the following questions using the cues provided. Follow the model.

Modelo ¿Qué me recomiendas? (tomar el tren)
Te recomiendo que tomes el tren.

1. ¿Qué les sugieres a los pasajeros? (facturar el equipaje)
_______________.

2. ¿Qué les dices a los turistas? (hacer reservaciones en un vuelo directo)
_______________.

3. ¿Qué quieres que yo haga? (planear el viaje conmigo)
_______________.

4. ¿Qué le sugieres a Pablo? (usar mi teléfono)
_______________.

5. ¿Qué te recomienda la agente de viajes? (llegar mucho antes de la salida del vuelo)
_______________.

6. ¿Qué les dices a los pasajeros? (no llevar tanto equipaje)
_______________.

7. ¿En qué cosa insiste el agente? (decirle lo que nos interesa)
_______________.

8. ¿Qué les recomiendas a los turistas? (venir temprano por la mañana)
_______________.

Nombre ______ Hora ______

Fecha ______ Practice Workbook **8A–6**

¿Qué deben hacer?

Señor Estrada is advising his students about their upcoming trip to Madrid. Select the best response from the word bank and answer the students' questions in complete sentences. Follow the model.

Modelo ¿Cómo debemos portarnos durante el viaje?

Chicos, quiero que *Uds. sean responsables*.

~~ser responsable~~	darme tu pasaporte para verlo
ir en avión	saber lo que van a hacer todos los días
saber el horario de los aviones	ir a Toledo
darme tu dirección en Madrid	ser buenos turistas
estar en el aeropuerto dos horas antes de la salida del vuelo	

1. —¿Cómo debemos viajar?

   —Madrid está lejos. Les recomiendo que ______.

2. —No sabemos qué aviones hay para Madrid.

   —Chicos, les sugiero que ______.

3. —¿Ud. me puede escribir una carta, profesor?

   —Sí, Amalia. Quiero que ______.

4. —¿Cuándo debemos llegar al aeropuerto?

   —Bueno, prefiero que ______.

5. —Creo que mi pasaporte está bien, pero no estoy segura.

   —En ese caso, Margarita, necesito que ______.

6. —¿Necesitamos planear bien nuestro viaje?

   —Sí. Insisto en que ______.

7. —¿Qué otras ciudades debemos visitar?

   —Recomiendo que ______.

8. —¿Cree Ud. que este viaje será un éxito?

   —Sí, chicos, quiero que ______.

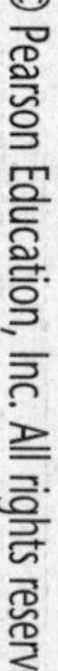

Go Online WEB CODE jdd-0805
PHSchool.com

Nombre ______________________ Hora __________

Fecha ______________________ Practice Workbook **8A–7**

El día de la salida

The Galíndez family is getting ready to go on a trip. Use the cues provided to write what they are telling each other to do.

Modelo cerrar las maletas

Marta, quiero que *cierres las maletas*.

1. ser paciente

   Joselito, necesitamos que ______________________.

2. ir a casa de su amiga ahora

   Lucía y Manuelito, les prohíbo que ______________________.

3. saber los números de nuestros vuelos

   Paco, insisto en que ______________________.

4. buscar tu maleta ahora

   Mamá, sugiero que Papá ______________________.

5. estar listos ahora

   Roberto y Amalia, quiero que ______________________.

6. darle tu pasaporte a papá

   Lucía, prefiero que ______________________.

7. sacar más juguetes ahora

   Joselito, no permito que ______________________.

8. empezar a apagar las luces

   Alberto, recomiendo que ______________________.

Repaso

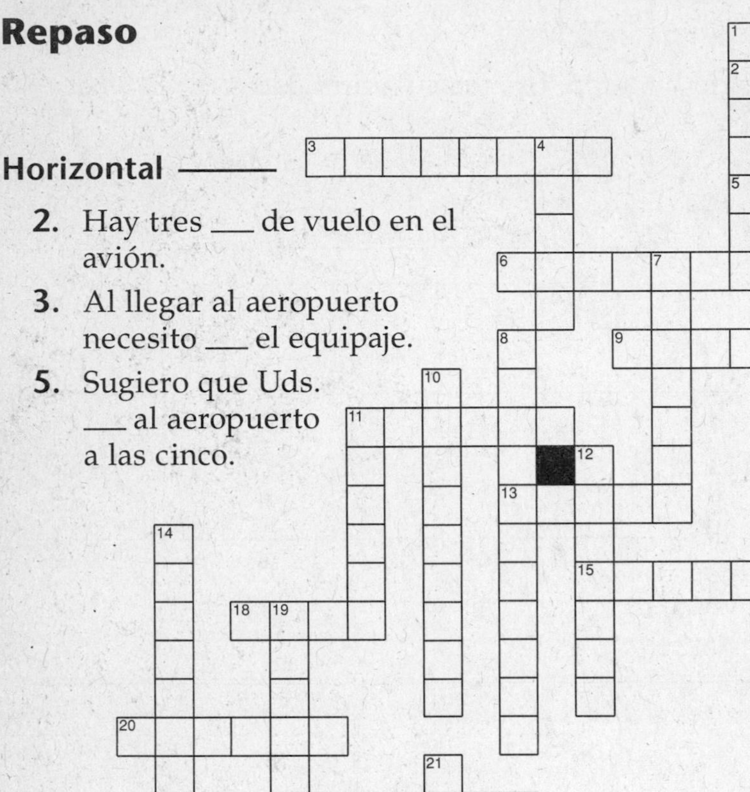

Horizontal

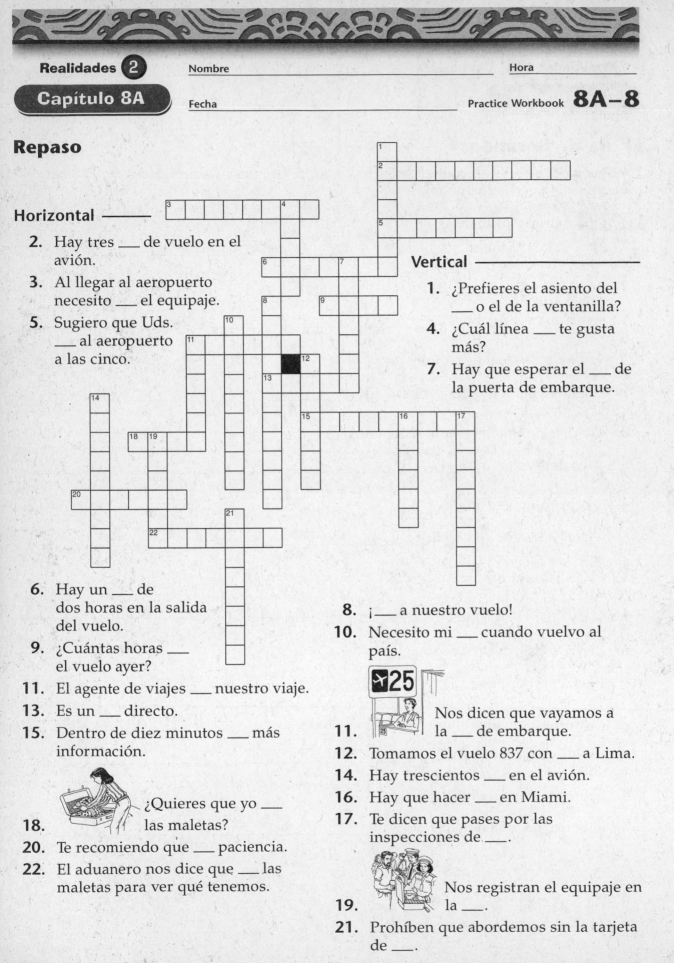

2. Hay tres ___ de vuelo en el avión.
3. Al llegar al aeropuerto necesito ___ el equipaje.
5. Sugiero que Uds. ___ al aeropuerto a las cinco.
6. Hay un ___ de dos horas en la salida del vuelo.
9. ¿Cuántas horas ___ el vuelo ayer?
11. El agente de viajes ___ nuestro viaje.
13. Es un ___ directo.
15. Dentro de diez minutos ___ más información.
18.  ¿Quieres que yo ___ las maletas?
20. Te recomiendo que ___ paciencia.
22. El aduanero nos dice que ___ las maletas para ver qué tenemos.

Vertical

1. ¿Prefieres el asiento del ___ o el de la ventanilla?
4. ¿Cuál línea ___ te gusta más?
7. Hay que esperar el ___ de la puerta de embarque.
8. ¡___ a nuestro vuelo!
10. Necesito mi ___ cuando vuelvo al país.
11. 

Nos dicen que vayamos a la ___ de embarque.
12. Tomamos el vuelo 837 con ___ a Lima.
14. Hay trescientos ___ en el avión.
16. Hay que hacer ___ en Miami.
17. Te dicen que pases por las inspecciones de ___.
19.  Nos registran el equipaje en la ___.
21. Prohíben que abordemos sin la tarjeta de ___.

Realidades 2 | Nombre _______________ | Hora _______

Capítulo 8A | Fecha _______________ | Practice Workbook **8A–9**

Organizer

I. Vocabulary

Items you need for a trip

Words to talk about making travel plans

Words to talk about airports

II. Grammar

1. When do you use the subjunctive mood?

   ____

2. The subjunctive mood is formed in the same way as the _______________ commands.

3. Give the present subjunctive forms of these verbs.

ir

ser

dar

saber

Go Online WEB CODE jdd-0808 PHSchool.com

Realidades 2 | Nombre ______ | Hora ______

Capítulo 8B | Fecha ______ | Practice Workbook **8B–1**

Haciendo una gira

Tell what these people are doing while on a tour during their vacation.

1. Mateo y Jacinta visitan el ______________________ donde viven los ______________________.
2. Emilia saca dinero del ______________________.
3. Nos encanta navegar en un ______________________.
4. Yo visité esta bella ______________________.
5. Los turistas prestan atención a la ______________________.
6. Diana le da ______________________ al joven que llevó su equipaje.
7. Tú y yo disfrutamos de hacer ______________________.
8. No es bueno hacer ______________________ en la habitación del hotel.
9. A los chicos les gusta ______________________.

Conversación: Dos turistas en Madrid

Read the conversation between Ana and Lola about their tour of Spain and then answer the questions.

ANA: Es bueno llegar temprano para poder empezar a conocer Madrid.

LOLA: De acuerdo. Según el itinerario, nos quedamos en Madrid cinco días pero creo que son pocos para verlo todo.

ANA: Quizás, pero hacemos una gira de toda la ciudad, entonces es bastante.

LOLA: Espero que vayamos al Palacio Real. ¡Quiero conocer al Rey!

ANA: ¡Qué cómica eres! Sí, vamos al palacio y después al Museo del Prado.

LOLA: Estupendo. Quiero ver esos bellos cuadros de Velázquez, el Greco y Goya. Necesitamos volver otro día para ver todo el museo.

ANA: Y para cenar nos llevan a un restaurante famoso que está en la Plaza Mayor. Si hace buen tiempo podemos comer al aire libre. Estoy muy emocionada.

LOLA: Según el itinerario, nos llevan a El Escorial el miércoles. Necesito leer un libro sobre el rey Felipe II y su palacio.

ANA: Y antes de ir a Toledo el día siguiente, voy a leer un libro sobre esta gran ciudad histórica.

LOLA: Dicen que la catedral más grande de España está en Toledo.

ANA: Es por eso que debemos leer más, no sólo sobre Madrid, pero sobre todo el país.

----

1. ¿Por qué dice Ana que cinco días es bastante para verlo todo en Madrid?

   ______________________________.

2. ¿Qué hay en el Palacio Real? ¿Cómo sabes?

   ______________________________.

3. Según el itinerario, ¿cuántos lugares van a ver en su primer día en Madrid?

   ______________________________.

4. ¿A Lola le gusta el arte español? ¿Cómo sabes?

   ______________________________.

5. ¿Las muchachas pueden disfrutar de la comida española? ¿En dónde?

   ______________________________.

6. ¿Sobre qué rey famoso van a aprender en el Escorial?

   ______________________________.

7. Según el itinerario, ¿cuántos días pasan entre su excursión a Toledo y la del Escorial?

   ______________________________.

8. ¿Qué monumento famoso hay en Toledo?

   ______________________________.

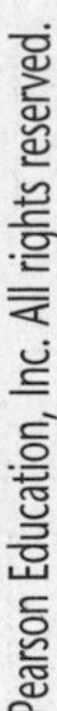

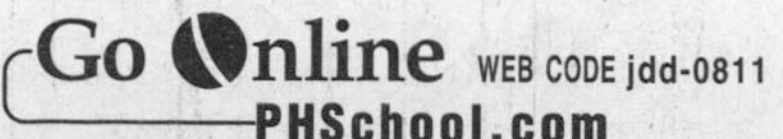

¿Qué es esto?

Read each of the following clues and write the vocabulary word or expression that is being described. Follow the model.

Modelo Es un edificio histórico, más grande que una iglesia. *una catedral*

1. Es otra manera de decir "quizás". ______
2. A veces esta persona se enoja cuando tratas de regatear en su tienda. ______
3. Para no ofender soy así con la gente. ______
4. Una persona puntual llega a la hora... ______
5. Es otra manera de decir "bonita". ______
6. Lo que haces en una casa de cambio. ______
7. Si no tienes dinero para alquilar una habitación doble, debes pedir una... ______
8. Tienes que conseguir la llave de tu habitación en la... ______
9. Si no puedes usar la escalera, debes preguntar si hay un... ______
10. Es otra manera de decir "divertirse". ______
11. Una persona que presta mucha atención es muy... ______
12. Para hacer esto en un lugar, normalmente necesitas una guía. ______

Go Online WEB CODE jdd-0812
PHSchool.com

Nombre ______________________ Hora ______________

Fecha ______________________

Ayudando a los turistas

You work at a tourist information center, and tourists have lots of questions today. Use the drawings to answer the questions in complete sentences. Follow the model.

Modelo  No sabemos qué hacer ahora. ¿Qué quiere Ud. que visitemos?

Quiero que visiten la catedral.

1. Buscamos una guía. ¿Dónde recomienda Ud. que la consigamos?

   ____.

2. ¿Qué me sugieres que haga en los mercados? No conozco la costumbre.

   ____.

3. ¿Qué me recomienda Ud.? Quiero comprar algo típico del país.

   ____.

4. Quiero escribirles a mis amigos, pero no tengo mucho tiempo. ¿Qué me sugiere Ud.?

   ____.

5. No podemos pagar dos habitaciones individuales. ¿Qué clase de habitación sugiere Ud. que pidamos?

   ____.

6. Hemos visto muchas catedrales. ¿Qué recomienda Ud. que visitemos ahora?

   ____.

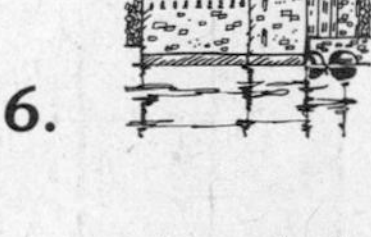

7. Tengo dólares pero no tengo euros. ¿Adónde sugiere que yo vaya?

   ____.

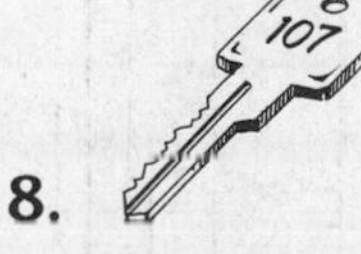

8. No podemos entrar en nuestra habitación. ¿Qué necesitamos que el empleado nos dé?

   ____.

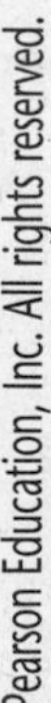

Realidades 2 | Nombre ______ | Hora ______

Capítulo 8B | Fecha ______ | Practice Workbook **8B–5**

Es bueno viajar

A. Choose from the verbs in parentheses to complete the expressions about travel. Underline the correct verb and write the appropriate form in the space provided. Follow the model.

Modelo Es bueno que nosotros *observemos* las costumbres. (observar / ofender)

1. Es importante que Octavia ______ una gira. (cambiar / hacer)
2. Es necesario que nosotros ______ dinero en la casa de cambio. (cambiar / navegar)
3. Es mejor que Uds. ______ al palacio por la mañana. (ser / ir)
4. Es bueno que yo ______ al aeropuerto a tiempo. (llegar / regatear)
5. Es importante que tú ______ los lugares históricos. (saber / conocer)
6. Es necesario que Manolo ______ atento a las explicaciones de la guía. (estar / hacer)

B. Now, use an impersonal expression to create a sentence with the words given. Follow the model.

Modelo los niños / ser cortés *Es bueno que los niños sean corteses*.

1. los turistas / no hacer ruido en la catedral

   ______.

2. yo / salir a las ocho en punto

   ______.

3. tú / hacer la gira por la mañana

   ______.

4. el profesor / disfrutar del tiempo libre

   ______.

5. nosotros / conseguir un pasaporte

   ______.

Realidades 2 Nombre ____________ Hora ________

Capítulo 8B Fecha ____________ Practice Workbook **8B–6**

Organizando las actividades

You are organizing a tour for a large group of tourists. Give the tourists advice based on the problems below. Choose an appropriate solution from the word bank and follow the model.

Modelo No quiero llevar tanto dinero en efectivo.

Entonces es necesario que *consigas una tarjeta de crédito*.

~~conseguir una tarjeta de crédito~~	entender un poco de español
cerrar las ventanas	pedir más agua
jugar al fútbol en el parque	dormir un poco
recordar la dirección del hotel	sentarse unos minutos
no perder la llave	vestirse ahora mismo

1. Todavía tengo sed.

   Entonces sugiero que ______________________________.

2. Los chicos dicen que tienen sueño.

   Entonces es bueno que ______________________________.

3. Vamos a tener que entrar en nuestra habitación.

   Entonces es importante que ______________________________.

4. Hemos caminado tanto que nos duelen los pies.

   Entonces es mejor que ______________________________.

5. Las niñas todavía no están vestidas.

   Entonces es necesario que ______________________________.

6. Los invitados tienen frío.

   Entonces sugiero que ______________________________.

7. Queremos volver al hotel sin problemas.

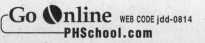

   Entonces es mejor que ______________________________.

8. Los muchachos quieren hacer un poco de deporte.

   Entonces recomiendo que ______________________________.

9. Queremos conocer a la gente.

   Entonces es mejor que ______________________________.

Go Online WEB CODE jdd-0814 PHSchool.com

Nombre ______________________ Hora ______________

Fecha ______________________ Practice Workbook **8B–7**

Estoy de acuerdo

Write complete sentences to agree with each of the statements below. Follow the model.

Modelo Yo creo que pueden venir. (es bueno)

Es bueno que puedan venir.

1. Siempre vuelven temprano. (es mejor)

 ______________________________.

2. Todos almuerzan aquí. (preferimos)

 ______________________________.

3. Todo el mundo recuerda la hora de la cena. (es importante)

 ______________________________.

4. Quieren ver la catedral. (es bueno)

 ______________________________.

5. Se despiden de sus amigos. (insistimos en)

 ______________________________.

6. Siguen las instrucciones del guía. (es importante)

 ______________________________.

7. Nadie pierde su pasaporte. (no quiero)

 ______________________________.

8. Todo el mundo se divierte. (quiero)

 ______________________________.

9. Los turistas se despiertan temprano. (es necesario)

 ______________________________.

10. Pido la tortilla española. (recomiendas)

 ______________________________.

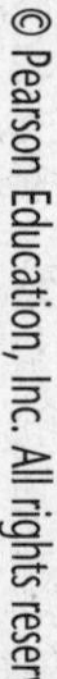

Go Online WEB CODE jdd-0816
PHSchool.com

Realidades 2 | Nombre _______ | Hora _______

Capítulo 8B | Fecha _______ | Practice Workbook **8B–8**

Repaso

Horizontal

4. ¿Te gusta ___ en bote de vela?
6. El ___ Felipe II vivía en El Escorial.
7. Los reyes viven en el ___.
8. Nos gusta montar en la ___ acuática.
9. Es importante que tú no ___ a nadie.
10. El autobús sale a la una en ___. 
11. Te dan la llave en la ___.
13. Es bueno que tú ___ una gira en mayo.
14. Compro periódicos y revistas en el ___.
15. Es bueno que tú ___ un trabajo de guía.
17. Siguen un ___ de quince días.
18. Espero que Uds. ___ de la gira. 
19. Esta ___ es típica del país.
20. Le dimos una ___ al camarero.
21. el ___; *elevator*

Vertical

1. Es mejor que Uds. no ___ con el vendedor.
2. Lee la ___ para saber más sobre los castillos españoles.
3. Cambio dinero en el ___ automático.
5. ¿Ud. necesita una ___ doble o individual?
10. Se venden tarjetas ___ en el quiosco.
11. Es importante que Uds. no hagan ___.
12. Es necesario que Ud. sea ___, que no llegue tarde. 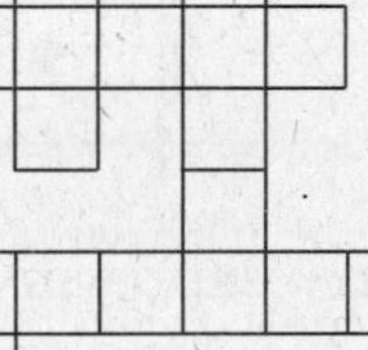
15.  Es una ___ grande.
16. Los turistas están ___ a lo que les dice el guía.

Nombre ______ Hora ______

Fecha ______ Practice Workbook **8B–9**

Organizer

I. Vocabulary

Places to visit in a city

Verbs/Phrases for things to do on trips

Words/Phrases about hotels

Words describing tourist behaviors

II. Grammar

1. Name four impersonal expressions that are often followed by the subjunctive.

2. How are **-ar** and **-er** stem-changing verbs different from **-ir** stem-changing verbs in the subjunctive?

3. Give the present subjunctive of these verbs:

recordar

perder

pedir

dormir

Go Online WEB CODE jdd-0817
PHSchool.com

Realidades 2 | Nombre ______ | Hora ______

Capítulo 9A | Fecha ______ | Practice Workbook **9A–A**

A ver si recuerdas...

El mundo natural

Complete the following sentences based on the drawings.

1. Alfredo estudia los ______________ y las ______________ en un parque nacional.

2. Yo recojo las ______________ de ______________ en el parque.

3. Emilia y Ernesto esquían en las ______________.

4. Es importante también reciclar las ______________.

5. Los estudiantes separan ______________ y ______________.

6. Margarita mira los ______________ en el parque.

7. Yo sigo las instrucciones del ______________.

8. Es importante reciclar el ______________ roto porque es peligroso.

9. Los chicos nadan en ______________.

Realidades 2 — Nombre ______ Hora ______

Capítulo 9A — Fecha ______ Practice Workbook **9A–B**

A ver si recuerdas...

Reciclando

Use the cues provided to answer the questions about what people do to help the environment. Follow the model.

Modelo ¿Qué hace Alejandro en el centro de reciclaje? (seguir instrucciones)
Sigue las instrucciones del centro de reciclaje.

1. ¿Qué haces tú en casa? (recoger periódicos)
______.
2. ¿Qué hago yo en el parque? (conseguir botellas de plástico)
(Tú) ______.
3. ¿Qué hacen Juan y Elena en el club? (enviar cartas a los políticos)
______.
4. ¿Qué hace Marta en la universidad? (seguir estudiando las ciencias naturales)
______.
5. ¿Qué hacen Raúl y Bárbara en casa? (no destruir el papel)
______.
6. ¿Qué haces tú en la comunidad? (escoger lugares para tirar el vidrio roto)
______.
7. ¿Qué hacen los trabajadores en el centro de reciclaje? (separar el plástico y el vidrio)
______.
8. ¿Qué hacen ustedes en la comunidad? (trabajar como voluntarios)
______.
9. ¿Qué hace Inés en la comunidad? (recoger la ropa usada)
______.
10. ¿Qué haces tú en casa? (reciclar las botellas)
______.

Go Online WEB CODE jdd-0901 PHSchool.com

¿Qué profesión tienen?

Based on the descriptions below, decide what each person does for a living.

Modelo A Felicia le gustan los animales. Ella es ___veterinaria___.

1. Lisa habla con mucha gente importante y discute productos nuevos para su compañía. Ella es ______________.
2. A Roberto le interesa la construcción de puentes y edificios. Él es ______________.
3. Rogelio va a trabajar en el campo con las plantas. Él va a ser ______________.
4. Nora envía cartas y paquetes todo el día. Ella es ______________.
5. A los hermanos Solís les gustan las matemáticas y les interesa construir edificios. Son ______________.
6. Mirna estudió derecho y ya era abogada. Ahora ella es ______________.
7. Marcelo repara coches. Es ______________.
8. Carmen trabaja en una compañía internacional, hablando por teléfono y escribiendo cartas. Ella es ______________.
9. Florencia trabaja en un laboratorio químico. Es ______________.
10. Julio estudia la ley en la universidad porque quiere ser ______________ y luego ______________.
11. Serena sabe mucho de las computadoras y trabaja con ellas todos los días. Ella es ______________.
12. Vicente les dice a otros qué hacer cada día. Es el ______________ de los empleados en una tienda.

Nombre ______ Hora ______

Fecha ______ Practice Workbook **9A–2**

¿Qué piensas estudiar?

Find out what Mildred, Lorena, Octavio, and Rafael want to study by completing their conversation with the words that correspond to the pictures in the bank.

MILDRED: Bueno, chicos, nos graduaremos el año que viene. ¿Saben qué ______ ______ van a tomar en ______?

LORENA: Bueno, yo pienso estudiar historia y ciencias sociales. Y después de ______ de la universidad pienso seguir estudiando derecho porque quiero ser ______ y algún día ______.

OCTAVIO: A mí me interesan muchas cosas. Si voy a la universidad pienso estudiar las matemáticas. Me gustaría ser ______. También me gustaría ser ______ porque me interesan los cursos donde aprendo de computadoras.

RAFAEL: Pienso tomar muchas clases de ciencias. Después de graduarme de la universidad pienso estudiar medicina. Me gustaría ser ______ y trabajar en un laboratorio. También me gustan los animales. Entonces puedo ser también ______. Y tú, Mildred, ¿qué piensas estudiar?

MILDRED: Yo no sé qué carrera voy a seguir. Por eso voy a tomar clases de ciencias, matemáticas, artes e idiomas. Para saber de todo.

LORENA: Entonces puedes ser ______ porque ellos saben de todo y a ellos les gusta hablar como tú.

Go Online WEB CODE jdd-0902
PHSchool.com

Cómo ganarse la vida

A. Read the following segment from Álvaro's essay that he has written about what kind of work he wants to do. Fill in the blanks with words from your vocabulary. Each dash represents a letter.

Yo quiero ganarme l(4) ___(15) ___(16) ___(20) ___(1) ___(15) como ___(1) u(25) ___(10) ___(21) o(5) de mi propio negocio. Me gustaría tener mi propia o(5) ___(13) ___(20) c(6) ___(20) ___(11) ___(15). También, quiero tomar mis propias decisiones, como cuál es el ___(7) ___(15) l(4) ___(15) ___(2) ___(20) o(5) de mis empleados y cuáles son sus b(3) ___(10) ___(11) ___(10) ___(13) ___(20) c(6) ___(20) o(5) ___(7) de salud. Me gustaría tener un secretario o una secretaria que hable más que dos ___(20) ___(1) ___(20) o(5) ___(19) ___(15) ___(7), como una secretaria brasileña que hable portugués, español y francés.

Para seguir esta c(6) ___(15) ___(2) ___(2) ___(10) ___(2) ___(15) pienso estudiar un poco después de recibir mi diploma. Quiero tomar unos cursos en la u(25) ___(11) ___(20) ___(16) ___(10) ___(2) ___(7) ___(20) ___(1) ___(15) ___(1). Sobre todo, quiero estudiar ___(11) ___(10) ___(17) o(5) c(6) ___(20) o(5) ___(7) porque necesito saber tanto como sea posible de lo que está pasando en mi ___(9) ___(2) o(5) ___(13) ___(10) ___(7) ___(20) ó(14) ___(11) como hombre de negocios.

B. Each letter from Part A has a number that corresponds to it. Fill in the letters to answer the question.

—¿Cuándo va a empezar la carrera de Álvaro?

—___(1) ___(10) ___(7) ___(9) ___(25) é(23) ___(7) ___(1) ___(10) ___(17) ___(2) a(15) ___(1) ___(25) a(15) ___(2) ___(7) ___(10) ___(1) ___(10) l(4) a(15) ___(25) ___(11) ___(20) v(16) ___(10) ___(2) ___(7) ___(20) ___(1) a(15) ___(1).

Nombre ______________________ Hora ______________

Fecha ______________________ Practice Workbook **9A–4**

Un futuro interesante

A. Tell whether each of the following statements is **cierto** or **falso.** If it is false, rewrite it to make it true. Use the art to help you. Follow the model.

Modelo Carla quiere seguir una carrera de artes.
Falso. Carla quiere seguir una carrera de negocios.

1. Jorge quiere seguir una carrera de tecnología.
____.

2. Linda quiere seguir una carrera militar.
____.

3. Tito quiere seguir una carrera de negocios.
____.

4. Catrina quiere estudiar las ciencias para su profesión.
____.

5. Manolo quiere seguir una carrera de artes.
____.

6. Teresa quiere seguir una carrera de tecnología.
____.

B. Now, complete the following analogies based on what you know about professions. Follow the model.

Modelo el artista : las artes :: el científico : *la tecnología*

1. la contadora : los negocios :: la abogada : ______________
2. los edificios : la arquitecta :: los animales : ______________
3. el cartero : el correo :: el secretario : ______________
4. el contador : un hombre de negocios :: el pintor : ______________
5. el empleado : el gerente :: el gerente : ______________

Quiero saber qué haces

Complete the responses to the following questions. Follow the model.

Modelo ¿Alfredo va a ser contador?
Sí, yo creo que *será contador*.

1. ¿Tu hermana va a seguir una carrera de negocios?
   Sí, me parece que ______________________.
2. ¿Juan Carlos va a trabajar de cartero?
   Sí, creo que ______________________.
3. ¿Va a haber muchas oportunidades para usar el español?
   Sí, pienso que ______________________.
4. ¿Tus primos van a graduarse este año?
   Sí, estoy seguro de que ______________________.
5. ¿Uds. van a escoger un programa de estudios?
   Sí, ______________________ el año siguiente.
6. ¿Tú vas a dibujar en la computadora?
   Sí, creo que ______________________.
7. ¿Yo comprenderé el mundo de las artes?
   Sí, yo sé que ______________________.
8. ¿Pedro y Carlota se van a casar?
   Sí, yo digo que ______________________.
9. ¿Uds. van a asistir a la universidad?
   Sí. Como sacamos buenas notas, ______________________.

Realidades 2

Capítulo 9A

Nombre ____________________ Hora ________

Fecha ____________________ Practice Workbook **9A–6**

Algún día

Read each of the problems below. Then, use the clues provided to tell each person what the future holds. Follow the model.

Modelo Ahora me es difícil conseguir trabajo. (encontrar un buen trabajo)
Algún día *tú encontrarás un buen trabajo* .

1. Todavía no he decidido qué cursos tomar. (saber qué quieres estudiar)
   Algún día ____.
2. No hay mucho trabajo ahora. (haber trabajos interesantes)
   Algún día ____.
3. Los Dávila quieren ser técnicos. (tener que asistir a una escuela técnica)
   Algún día ____.
4. Quiero que tú y yo vayamos a comer al campo. (hacer un picnic)
   Algún día ____.
5. Nuestros primos nunca nos visitan. (poder venir a vernos)
   Algún día ____.
6. Siempre tenemos tanta prisa tú y yo que no podemos hacer nada. (tener tiempo para todo)
   Algún día ____.
7. Te es muy difícil aprender las palabras nuevas. (saber todo el vocabulario)
   Algún día ____.
8. No hay muchos profesores en nuestro colegio. (haber más profesores)
   Algún día ____.
9. Tengo que buscar trabajo. No puedo seguir estudiando después de graduarme. (poder ir a la universidad)
   Algún día ____.
10. Hace diez años que no eres el personaje principal. (hacer el papel del galán)
    Algún día ____.

Go Online WEB CODE jdd-0905
PHSchool.com

Los primeros días en la universidad

Ricardo has just arrived at the university where his cousin Manuel is a third-year student. Complete their conversation with the future tense of the verbs in parentheses. The first one has been done for you.

RICARDO: ¡Qué grande es la universidad, Manuel! Seguro que *me perderé* (perderse) mucho.

MANUEL: No, no ______ (perderse). Pronto todo ______ (ser) normal para ti.

RICARDO: Y todavía necesito decidir qué clases ______ (tomar).

MANUEL: ______ (Tener) que hablar con un representante de la universidad. Él ______ (saber) lo que necesitas estudiar.

RICARDO: Y, ¿crees que ______ (estar) contento en mi habitación?

MANUEL: Estoy seguro de que te ______ (gustar) tu habitación.

RICARDO: ¿Piensas que yo ______ (poder) hacer toda la tarea?

MANUEL: Claro que sí. Siempre has sido un buen estudiante. No ______ (haber) problema.

RICARDO: No conozco a nadie aquí. ¿Qué ______ (hacer) para divertirme?

MANUEL: Tú ______ (conocer) a mucha gente y ______ (divertirse) mucho. Yo te ______ (presentar) a todos mis amigos. Nosotros ______ (ir) a muchos lugares juntos.

RICARDO: Gracias, Manuel. Ya tengo menos miedo que antes.

MANUEL: No tienes por qué estar nervioso. Yo sé que ______ (tener) mucho éxito en la universidad.

Repaso

Horizontal

2. Estos ___ trabajan con las computadoras.
3. Jaime estudiará para ___ porque le gustan las ciencias.
7. Los edificios de esta ___ son los más interesantes de la ciudad.
8. Este abogado quiere ser ___ algún día.
9. ¿Cómo te ___ la vida?
11. Luis es ___.
14. Pepe va a la universidad o a una ___ técnica.
15. Tus cuadros son bellos. Eres un buen ___.
16. Mi trabajo es excelente, con un buen salario y ___.
17. A Pilar le gustan los animales. Será ___.
21. Roberto recibe un ___ muy bueno ahora.
22. El ___ acaba de entregarme las cartas.
23. ¿Qué ___ quieres seguir en la universidad?
24. Ricardo quiere ser abogado. Estudia ___.

Vertical

1. La secretaria habla inglés y español. Es ___.
4. Me ___ de la universidad el año que viene.
5. Consuelo seguirá un ___ de estudios en los negocios.
6. Daniel es ___ de su propio negocio.
10. ¿Qué harán Uds. en el ___?
12. Si quiere hablar con el gerente vaya a su ___.
13. Este hombre de ___ tiene mucho éxito.
18. Victoria ha escrito varios libros. Es una ___ famosa.
19. El ___ vende sus manzanas y tomates en el mercado.
20. ¿Estudias español u otro ___?

Nombre ______ Hora ______

Fecha ______ Practice Workbook **9A–9**

Organizer

I. Vocabulary

Professions in science and technology

______

Professions in law and politics

______

Professions in business

______

Words to talk about the future

______

II. Grammar

1. Give the future tense forms of these verbs.

trabajar

______

seguir

______

2. Give the **yo** form of the future tense of these verbs:

saber ______ **hacer** ______

poder ______ **tener** ______

El medio ambiente

Use the drawings to complete the following sentences about environmental problems.

1. El agua ______________________ es un problema grave en esta ciudad. No es buena para la salud.

2. Ciertos animales están en ______________________ de ______________________. Debemos protegerlos.

3. Se debe reducir el uso de ______________________. Necesitamos usar otras fuentes de energía.

4. Ocurre aire contaminado por casi todo el medio ______________________.

5. Puede haber contaminación en las ______________________.

6. Hay que proteger la belleza de ______________________, como los bosques y los desiertos.

7. Estos jóvenes participan en un grupo ______________________. Hablan de los problemas del medio ambiente.

8. Tenemos que luchar contra la contaminación de ______________________.

Go Online
WEB CODE jdd-0911
PHSchool.com

La ecología

A. Complete the following sentences by choosing the best verb and writing the correct form in the space provided. Follow the model.

Modelo Es necesario que los países *encuentren* otras fuentes de energía. (encontrar / eliminar)

1. Es importante que nosotros ________ los animales que están en peligro de extinción. (reducir / proteger)
2. Los científicos tratan de ________ la situación ecológica. (luchar / mejorar)
3. Es necesario que los miembros del grupo ecológico ________. (juntarse / resolver)
4. Muchos países ________ contra la destrucción del medio ambiente. (luchar / destruir)
5. Es necesario ________ la contaminación del aire. (proteger / eliminar)
6. Tenemos que ________ la contaminación del agua. (reducir / usar)
7. Es malo que sigamos ________ los bosques. (proteger / destruir)
8. El pueblo ________ el problema del agua contaminada. (resolver / luchar)

B. Complete the conversation between Paula and Marco about their environmental group. Not all of the words will be used.

luchar	**fuentes**	**nos juntamos**
medio ambiente	**grave**	**resolver**
reducir	**contaminación**	**ecológico**

PAULA: Hoy nosotros ________ con el grupo ________ de la comunidad, ¿verdad?

MARCO: Sí, es importante que haya una reunión todas las semanas porque tenemos muchos problemas que ________.

PAULA: Es cierto, Marco. Tenemos que ________ contra la destrucción de nuestro ________. Es un problema muy ________.

MARCO: Yo sé que Felipe querrá hablar de la contaminación del aire.

PAULA: Y Lidia piensa hablar de la ________ del agua. A Leonardo le interesa la idea de buscar otras ________ de energía.

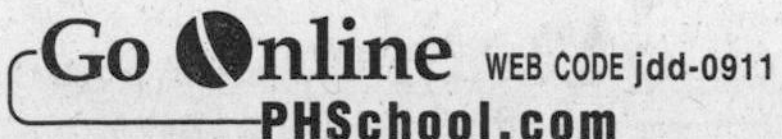

WEB CODE jdd-0911

Nombre ______ Hora ______

Fecha ______ Practice Workbook **9B–3**

La ecología y un mundo mejor

Read the following sentences carefully and complete them with the logical word or phrase.

Modelo En el metro viajan muchas personas. En el coche viajan pocas. El metro es más ___eficiente___.

1. Cuesta poco ir en autobús. El autobús es ______.
2. Hace tanto calor hoy. Tenemos que encender ______ para poder trabajar.
3. Siempre dejas las luces encendidas. Apágalas para ______ energía.
4. Hay mucha basura en este lago. No tiene agua ______.
5. Si reduces el uso de electricidad, vas a ______ dinero.
6. La energía solar viene del calor del sol. El sol puede ser una buena ______ de energía.
7. Hay mucha luz esta noche. No hay nubes y ______ está llena. ¡Es tan bonita!
8. Vivo en Jacksonville, Florida, pero en el invierno hace tanto frío que tengo que encender ______.
9. Muy cerca del ecuador en América del Sur, hay muchas ______ con plantas y árboles.
10. Ellos dejaron la gran ciudad para mudarse a un ______ pequeño.
11. Mucha gente muere durante las ______ entre los países.
12. Cuando un país no lucha contra otro, hay ______ entre los países.

Go Online WEB CODE jdd-0912 PHSchool.com

Nombre ____________________ Hora ________

Fecha ____________________

Problemas del medio ambiente

Answer the following questions in complete sentences based on the drawings.

1.  ¿Cuál es una de las causas más graves del calentamiento del mundo?

   ____.

2. 

   ¿Qué podemos hacer para conservar los bosques?

   ____.

3.  ¿Cuál es una manera de ahorrar la energía y reducir el aire contaminado?

   ____.

4.  ¿Qué es necesario para resolver los problemas políticos del mundo?

   ____.

5.  Si la Tierra se contamina demasiado, ¿qué más podemos hacer?

   ____.

6. 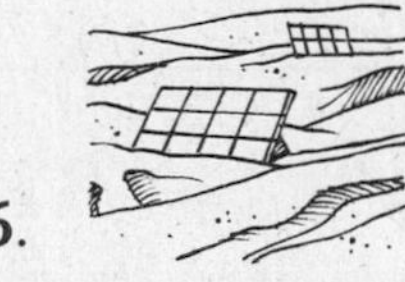 ¿Dónde es un lugar perfecto para usar la calefacción solar?

   ____.

7.  ¿Por qué es necesario reducir el uso del petróleo?

   ____.

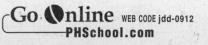

Nuestro medio ambiente en el futuro

Students are talking about what the environment is like today. They are pessimistic about tomorrow. Use the cues provided to tell what they think things will be like. Follow the model.

Modelo Hoy podemos nadar en este río.

El año que viene *no podremos nadar aquí* .

1. Hoy hay muchos bosques grandes.

   Dentro de 20 años ____________________ .

2. Hoy todos dicen que nuestra región es bonita.

   Dentro de cinco años ____________________ .

3. Hoy vienen muchos turistas a nuestras playas.

   Dentro de diez años ____________________ .

4. Hoy es posible eliminar la contaminación.

   El año que viene ____________________ .

5. Hoy muchos tienen calefacción solar.

   En el futuro ____________________ .

6. Hoy los estudiantes salen a recoger basura.

   La semana que viene ____________________ .

7. Hoy ponemos plantas en la sala de clases.

   El mes que viene ____________________ .

8. Hoy hacemos un esfuerzo por proteger el medio ambiente.

   Mañana ____________________ .

9. Hoy quiero ayudar a los otros estudiantes.

   Mañana ____________________ .

No estoy de acuerdo

Disagree with the following statements using the expressions of doubt in parentheses. Follow the model.

Modelo Estoy seguro que no protegen la selva tropical. (es imposible)
Es imposible que no protejan la selva tropical ______.

1. Creo que resuelven estos problemas ecológicos. (dudamos)
______.
2. Los estudiantes se juntan para conservar la naturaleza. (no creo)
______.
3. El grupo ecológico no tiene éxito. (es imposible)
______.
4. No reducen el uso de electricidad. (es posible)
______.
5. Creo que destruyen los bosques. (no creo)
______.
6. Dicen que estos animales están en peligro de extinción. (no estamos seguros)
______.
7. Piensan que hay soluciones fáciles. (no creemos)
______.
8. Creo que es difícil mejorar la situación del agua. (no es cierto)
______.
9. Dicen que se puede eliminar toda la contaminación. (dudo)
______.

Realidades 2 Nombre ______ Hora ______

Capítulo 9B Fecha ______ Practice Workbook **9B–7**

Conversando sobre el medio ambiente

Óscar el optimista and **Pilar la pesimista** are discussing environmental issues. Under each topic, write what each would say using the appropriate tense. Follow the model.

Modelo poder resolver el problema de la contaminación

ÓSCAR: *Yo digo que podrán resolver el problema de la contaminación en el futuro*.

PILAR: *Dudo que puedan resolver el problema de la contaminación en el futuro*.

1. salvar los animales

   ÓSCAR: ______.

   PILAR: ______.

2. reducir la contaminación

   ÓSCAR: ______.

   PILAR: ______.

3. mejorar el agua

   ÓSCAR: ______.

   PILAR: ______.

4. haber pocos problemas con el medio ambiente

   ÓSCAR: ______.

   PILAR: ______.

5. pasar leyes estrictas sobre la contaminación

   ÓSCAR: ______.

   PILAR: ______.

6. proteger los bosques

   ÓSCAR: ______.

   PILAR: ______.

7. haber menos contaminación del aire

   ÓSCAR: ______.

   PILAR: ______.

8. usar otras fuentes de energía

   ÓSCAR: ______.

   PILAR: ______.

Go Online WEB CODE jdd-0915 PHSchool.com

Repaso

Horizontal

8. La gente está preocupada por la ___ del aire.
11. Nuestros amigos viven en un ___ pequeño.
13. Hay que ___ contra la destrucción del medio ambiente.
14. La contaminación del aire es un problema ___.
18. Vamos a encender el aire ___.
19. Ciertos animales están en ___ de extinción.
20. Se encuentran plantas interesantes en la ___ tropical.
22. Es necesario ___ los problemas ecológicos.

Vertical

1. El aire acondicionado no ___ bien hoy.
2. Hay que ___ el uso de la electricidad.
3. Los chicos se ___ ayer para hablar de la guerra.
4. Se encuentra poca agua en el ___.
5. Es importante que busquemos otras ___ de energía.
6. La ___ se ve muy grande esta noche.
7. Los estudiantes hablan de la contaminación en su club ___.
9. Se habla mucho del ___ ambiente.
10. Otra fuente de energía es la ___ solar.
11. El agua que viene del bosque es muy ___.
12. Puedes ___ dinero si usas menos electricidad.
15. Tratan de ___ la contaminación del aire.
16. Es una ___ eficiente y económica de resolver el problema.
17. No se debe beber el agua ___.
19. Debemos ___ la belleza de la naturaleza.
21.  Se ve el ___ muy bien desde esta colina.

Nombre ______ Hora ______

Fecha ______ Practice Workbook **9B–9**

Organizer

I. Vocabulary

Words to talk about the landscape

______
______
______
______
______
______

Words to talk about energy

______
______
______
______
______
______

Nouns pertaining to the environment

______
______
______
______
______

Verbs pertaining to the environment

______
______
______
______
______

II. Grammar

1. Give the appropriate form of the future tense of these verbs.

   salir (yo) ______
   decir (tú) ______
   venir (Ud.) ______
   poner (Uds.) ______
   querer (nosotros) ______

2. Why do you use the subjunctive after **No es cierto que** but the indicative after **Es cierto que**?

   ______
   ______

3. List three expressions of doubt that are followed by the subjunctive.

   ______
   ______
   ______

Go Online WEB CODE jdd-0916
PHSchool.com